How GOD SPEAKS
to Ordinary People

Georgia Branscome

ISBN 978-1-63885-079-3 (Paperback)
ISBN 978-1-63885-080-9 (Digital)

Copyright © 2021 Georgia Branscome
All rights reserved
First Edition

All rights reserved. No part of this publication may be reproduced, distributed, or transmitted in any form or by any means, including photocopying, recording, or other electronic or mechanical methods without the prior written permission of the publisher. For permission requests, solicit the publisher via the address below.

Covenant Books, Inc.
11661 Hwy 707
Murrells Inlet, SC 29576
www.covenantbooks.com

A MESSAGE TO MY READERS

June 16, 2016, I made the call that would change our lives forever.

When the ambulance arrived, four men placed my husband, who was in the last stage of Parkinson's, in the ambulance. Never again would he see his home; never again would he work out in his garage.

Never again would our lives be the same.

I went from my father's house to become a wife almost sixty years ago and now alone for the first time.

Thanksgiving Day 2017, David was once again transferred, not by men but by His Savior.

It was truly a day of thanksgiving. Our grieving as we watched his suffering was replaced with a true day of Thanksgiving that our family celebrates every year.

As you read my writings, you may see I speak a lot about what I have learned since that time of trial.

It was during this time my faith grew. It was a painful time but a joyful time, a time where God showed me one of the most powerful lessons I have ever learned.

In the story of Patty, you will find it.

The main thing I feared was not being alone but that I would lose the close fellowship with God that had brought me such peace and comfort during such a tiring time for myself and my family.

When I became a widow, my earthly husband was no longer with me, but my heavenly husband has never left me.

I am never alone, and my wonderful Savior reveals Himself to me through His Bible, His beautiful creation, and the many wonderful ministers that are faithful to God's word.

I am excited about what is ahead. God tells me I may be eighty, but He isn't finished with me yet, and when He is, I too will be transferred to my forever home.

THE TENANT

It was a nice neighborhood. The streets were paved and wide enough so cars could be safely driven. Trees lined the streets, and in the spring, the fragrance of cherry blossoms filled the air. Children played on the sidewalks. The houses were pretty much the same. You could see a little difference, but most were well-kept. Yes, all in all, it was a very nice place to live.

Mrs. Jones lived in the house at 925 Alder Street. She kept up her house with great care. This is her story as she told it.

It was important to me that my house looked as good as those around me, so I took great care in keeping it that way. Even though I had lived there for many years, I knew how important appearance was. Up the hill was a house much nicer, and I wanted to someday have one just like that, so that became my goal; that is why I worked so hard. I knew my house was better than the one on the corner, and I took great pride in that. But the tenant that lived three doors down, Mrs. Kline, was a great irritation to me. She just never quit telling her story. It seems something happened inside her house that almost destroyed it. She and others tried to fix it and couldn't, then she heard about a man that could. It seemed he did, and that was all she talked about. She always wanted me to meet him, but it didn't interest me a bit.

As I said, I really took great pride in keeping up the outside of my house; at times it became an obsession. I was quite friendly with my neighbors, and I could tell they were impressed when they saw the way I was helping others. But one day, things started to change.

It was a Friday about eight o'clock, I remember it was in May, when someone knocked on the door of my house. I just didn't feel like answering it. My house was such a mess I wasn't about to let anyone see inside. So I didn't. As I looked around, I realized I was a hoarder. I had never seen that before. But it was late, so I just got busy for the next day.

It was a few days later when someone knocked. I was tired again. This time I opened the door just enough to tell the person I was not interested and shut the door.

I couldn't stop looking at the mess inside my house.

I became quite irritated when the knock came again. This time I just opened the door ready to say, "I am busy." But somehow, I don't know why, the words just came out. "I don't have much time, but come in for a minute."

Sure enough, it was Mrs. Kline's friend. I was embarrassed about the mess in my house, but He seemed to understand. He didn't stay long, and after His visit, I forgot all about it.

I was surprised when He came again. This time I listened. And I just started talking. It wasn't easy telling Him about myself. You see what people thought was so important, and there was no way I would ever let someone see inside my house.

I told Him I didn't even know who owned this house. I had never even paid any rent. And this mess inside was my fault; I brought it all in. It was then Mrs. Kline's friend told me who He was. He told me that my house was owned by Him. He made it just for me. He said if I would invite Him in, He would come to live with me. So I did. It was wonderful knowing I had a friend that had seen the inside and still wanted in.

That same day, He moved into my house. Each morning before work, we would sit and visit. I would tell Him about me, but most important, He came to reveal more about Himself to me. My heart would break one minute and, the next, burst with joy as He told me how much He had done for me.

This went on day after day, then one day, we took a walk through my house, and He showed me all I had hoarded. And it was time to clean the inside of my house. It was easy to get rid of some of my mess, but when it came to my trophy room, that took some time. That day, I saw the dust on my plaques of good deeds that had to go because by now I knew why I had done them—for me. So out they went. Next came pictures of some people. That was the hardest. You see, what they said and how they treated me, I never wanted to forget. Some, He said, I had to forgive because He couldn't help me until I forgive them. Well, the day came when I found I had. Oh, the hurt still lingered, but then He helped me. Next, that was beyond my strength. He said I couldn't love someone more than Him. There was one picture in a prominent place. I didn't know when I put that up, but I recognized myself. One day I could take it down; the next day I couldn't.

Some others were hard but came easier. Then He explained I had two enemies that didn't want me to have a clean house—my old self who wanted my way, and the one who came to rob, kill, and destroy, Satan.

Day after day, and sad to say much later, as we met each day, my love would grow stronger. I learned when I put Him as my first love, I loved others the way He taught me to.

It was then I went to Mrs. Kline, and we became good friends. She told me it wasn't easy for her to let go of what she wanted either. But when she did, she was amazed that she hadn't sooner.

The day came my trophy room was totally cleaned out, and I asked my friend Jesus to move in. He did.

It wasn't long after, a crack came into my house, and the enemy, my old self, tried to come into the trophy room. When I asked Jesus about that, He told me how Satan tried to tempt Him too and how He told him what the Father told Him to say, and that was what I did.

Now my house was filled with joy and contentment. Sometime later, there was a pounding on the door. I was shaking with fear. The enemy had come to rob everything in my house. I just cried out to Jesus and he went to the door and my enemy had to flee.

Yes, it is a wonderful place to live. The streets are wide. The children still play in the neighborhood. Cherry blossoms fill the air.

The big house on the hill is still there. The tenant is a wonderful man. His wife invited me to coffee the other day. I love her house, and I am so happy for her. We talked about Mrs. Kline's and my friend. Someday I'm hoping she will meet with Him too.

The house on the corner may not look as nice as mine, but I met that tenant too. She has known my friend for years. It's then I know how I just saw the outside and never the beauty inside.

The other day, Jesus reminded me this house I'm a tenant of is just temporary because He has prepared for me a mansion where I will live forever with Him. But until then, I am to keep my house clean inside and outside. Oh, yes, and He said His joy, peace, and contentment will keep filling every room.

THE DRESS

Each year, there is the celebrity walk. They arrive in their limousines, and as they walk down the carpet, an announcer is describing their one-of-a-kind dress with the emphasis on the famous designer.

It's not long before the hangers in the department stores are displaying what has become known as knockoffs, and many will be there wanting one.

We would be foolish to think our bodies would fit into their original dresses. It's just as foolish to think we can fit into someone else's original design.

Each of us has a designer, God our Father, who has made everyone an original, tailor-made just for each of us.

Remember God made you an original.

As you walk your journey in life, may all describe you always with the emphasis on your Designer.

That's a perfect fit.

READY OR NOT

The wisest people we know do not know what this day will bring. But God does, and He has already given us everything we need to live this day to the fullest.

During the Revolutionary War there, were civilian colonists who trained themselves to go into the battle at a moment's notice. We know them as the Minute Men.

As believers, we too are to be ready "to give the reason for our hope."

Just as the Minute Men trained themselves for battle, we are too. and we have the manual. It is called the Bible.

It is our choice to be ready with the full armor God has given us, but it is up to us to put it on.

Just as David used little stones to defeat a giant. we have the Rock that we have built our lives on.

Jesus, the Rock, keeps us steadfast so we can live in the peace of God that no one can fully understand.

We must all be a minute man, prepared and ready, and in the strength of God, we will be victorious. We must contend for the truth and remember there is always enough time to do God's work, today, one day at a time.

Victory is ours!

I HAVE A QUESTION

Children, don't you just love them.

I think after they first learn the word *no*, the next is *why*.

Their eager little faces look up as they look at a tiny bug and ask why do they do this or that, and as we try to explain, they once again ask why.

So I have a question.

Why do we make being a Christian so complicated? Isn't it just loving God above all and others like God loves us? Jesus said it so; it has to be true.

Why don't we believe our Savior and try to rationalize what we don't understand? Didn't He say His ways are not our ways?

Why don't we believe God is not limited and not trust that He can do the unimaginable? Didn't He say the whole earth and everything in it is His?

Why do we fear when He promised He will never leave us or forsake us?

I was just wondering why sometimes I ask God why is this happening when He already told me I will have problems, and I am never alone.

Just wondering, do you ask why too?

EXPECTATIONS

We are to love those who don't love us and those who are unbelievers. But don't even expect them to think or act like a believer. Remember what the Apostle Paul wrote, "We used to live and think that way too" (Ephesians 2:1–10).

We didn't and couldn't live as a believer until God did for us what we couldn't, when He in His Grace gave us a new nature when by faith we believed. Now the Holy Spirit gives us new desires and His strength, all because we were born again.

Aren't you thankful you were born again?

What a privilege it is to pray that others will accept the free gift of salvation, and then they will rejoice and sing with us the popular hymn "Born Again" with the words "I'm not ashamed there's really been a change in me / born again just like Jesus said / born again all because of Calvary / I'm so glad that I've been born again."

LORD OF THE MANOR

God has shown His love for mankind.

His love is shown by the creation of the world before man was even created. Genesis shows us how He created everything that has ever been created, all with great care. He made beauty to surround us, food for our bodies, and our spirits to commune with Him.

After all He created, "God saw all He made and it was very good" (Genesis 1:31).

We see God's love and care in John 3:16 when we are told "God so loved this world He gave His only begotten Son that whoever believes in Him will have eternal life." When we believe in Jesus's atoning death for our sin and His resurrection, He gives us a new nature, new desires, and He comes to live inside of us so we can live a life through His strength.

When He is the Lord of the manor (our lives), not just a visitor, He is welcome into our computer room (our thinking). He has free reign there. He is in our bedroom, our sensual life. He is in control of our hands and feet, what we do. He has access to all our money; after all, that's His too. We see with His eyes, our ears, what we listen to. Now everything belongs to Him. He has indeed become the Lord of our hearts. Nothing is held back; after all, there is only room for one on the throne, Jesus the King of kings.

Now His presence brings peace, joy, and contentment, and we can rejoice every day in every situation because the King is on the throne!

DUCK SEASON

Fall, such a beautiful time of the year. The trees are changing, and the weather is cooling. With the season change, the annual duck season arrives.

The hunters have planned for months. They arise way before dawn, dress in their camouflage clothes, and head out to the lakes to carry out their planning.

With decoys in place and hidden behind the blind with their faithful dog beside them, they patiently wait.

At the crack of dawn, the unsuspecting ducks are flying overhead with their plans to land on their place of destination, the lake.

Two separate plans. Whose plan will succeed?

With careful aim, the hunter can succeed only if the ducks are flying low or sitting on the water.

It's not easy for the ducks to fly high. They don't glide but work their wings to reach safety. At the first shot, they go higher and higher.

It's a good lesson for us.

We too have an enemy out to get us, and it's not just an annual season; it's open season all year long. And just as the hunters put on camouflage to deceive the duck, so Satan hides his evil plans to rob and kill.

So take a lesson from the ducks. When an attack comes, we don't need to be sitting ducks but should climb higher into God's protection.

ADAPTERS

We are told by the culture today we are to adapt or be politically correct.

I hear many say I just want to go back to normal.

I have a question. What was normal?

The Hebrew children being led out of Egypt, of slavery, became so used to it that they said, "We want to go back. We had leeks and onions." But they forgot they were slaves.

I don't want to go back. Just as Paul said, "But one thing I do: Forgetting what is behind and straining toward what is ahead" (Philippians 3:13 NIV) so should we, but we should also remember what is in the past.

Our country has killed many babies in the last forty-seven years, over sixty-two million. Our country now recognizes homosexual marriage.

Violence covers the land.

Children have lost their innocence through the schools and internet.

Our government leaders are full of greed.

Our churches (not all) do not teach the truth but appeal to the greed and comfort of life. No, I don't want to go back to what was normal.

I want our country to repent, each one of us, and seek God, and when we do, we will not want to go back to adapting to the culture, but we will look ahead to what God will do. Then just maybe, instead of wanting to look back, we will look forward to what lies ahead.

Our lives are too short to look back. Look to what lies ahead— eternity with Jesus!

We sing the hymn "I have decided to follow Jesus / the world behind me, the cross before me / thou none go with me I will follow." That should be our decision. *No* turning back.

LISTEN TO TRUTH

God speaks to us in many ways.

We are told we are to seek knowledge, wisdom, and discernment.

The more we know God's truth, the more we understand and the more we are able to see and reject false teaching.

We have observed how many churches have leaned on man's wisdom and rejected the living word of God.

Israel was turning from the true prophets of God and listening to the false prophets because they refused the truth; just as our country is.

We are told of a king in the Scripture who, before going into battle, called these false prophets because he knew they would tell him what he wanted to hear. When he was asked to call a true prophet that only spoke God's instruction, the king said he didn't want to because he only spoke words he didn't want to hear. When he followed the advice of the false prophets, he was killed in battle.

But we read also of the Prophet Daniel, whom God spoke to directly, who listened to a true prophet, Jeremiah, and learned what the people were to do.

Another servant of God, Paul, who learned from a great teacher, Gamaliel, learned head knowledge, but it was by an encounter with God on the road to Damascus that with God's wisdom and under the leadership of the Holy Spirit, he wrote most of the New Testament.

We are a blessed generation. We have Bibles, devotionals, faithful ministers, and the Holy Spirit to lead us to the truth of God.

Yes, we must keep on learning; we must keep searching the Scriptures. Most of all, we must learn to obey God.

We are warned not to have itchy ears, listening to what we want to hear. We must only listen to the true truth that is as true today as it was yesterday and will still be true tomorrow.

We have much to learn, but we must listen only to those who teach the true word of God.

OLD SHEP

When my kids were little, I used to sing to them.

One song was "Walking to Missouri (Poor Little Robin)." It was a song by Sammy Kaye. It was a story about a poor little robin that couldn't afford to fly. It really was a metaphor for a prodigal that left his home in Missouri, and he was returning home heartbroken and broke.

One of their most requested was "Old Shep," a Red Foley song from 1933.

The story tells about his German shepherd dog named Hoover, his faithful dog since he was a lad, how they roamed over the countryside, just a boy and his dog. They were both full of fun. Once, Shep jumped into a pond and saved him from drowning.

Years went by, and Shep was now old when the doctor said, "I can do no more for him."

This is what made my kids cry. The words "Now Old Shep is gone / where the good doggies go / but if dogs have a heaven / there's one thing I know / Old Shep has a wonderful home."

The prodigal (poor little robin) knew he could go home just as the story in the Bible tells us. The prodigal son went home where his father ran and greeted him with love.

Tears would run down their little faces but rejoiced when the words assured them Old Shep was such a faithful dog, he would be in heaven.

We are told we have a friend that sticks closer than a brother, Jesus, our faithful friend, that goes with us wherever we go, even when we return broken.

Yes, Jesus is faithful even when we aren't.

All the songs in my story can be heard by looking up on the internet.

IT'S AN INSIDE JOB

Spring housecleaning is a tradition.

We open up the windows to allow the fresh breath of spring in.

We gather our supplies, and with great determination, we tackle the job. Where do we start? Isn't it usually what we can see?

But God's housecleaning is different from mine. He cleans up the inside first because He knows when the inside is clean, we can't stand the outside being dirty.

God alone knows the inside of our hearts and minds. But He alone knows how to cleanse us. He so gently shows us what we have hidden in the closets of our minds. He knows the hurts that has caused the bitterness to grow. He knows the masks we wear. But He also knows we can't clean up our lives. We may try, but it is just temporary.

God, our loving Father, knows what each of us need, and in His strength, He makes the inside clean.

Jesus, speaking to the religious leaders of the time, told them, "Woe to you, hypocrites, you clean the outside of the cup and dish, but inside they are full of greed and self-indulgence. Blind Pharisees first clean the inside of the cup and dish then the outside will also be clean" (Matthew 23:26 NIV).

God wants to clean inside our hearts. His desire for us never changed. First, the inside, then the outside will be clean.

Just as we open the windows to allow the fresh air in, we have to open our heart to the Holy Spirit, allowing Him to do His work inside.

I am thankful as Paul said, "Being confident of this, that he who began a good work in you will carry it on to completion until the day of Christ Jesus."

HOW WONDERFUL IS LOVE LIKE THIS

The biggest and most profound mystery to me is Jesus, all God, yet all human. Scripture tells us Jesus learned obedience. His body suffered, and He was tempted like we are, and yet He didn't sin. All I know is all that is true, and I will and can't understand.

Jesus allowed Himself to become human. In the book of Genesis, we are told He created everything beautiful just for us. Everything we needed, He provided before He created man. We are even told He gave His life by crucifixion before creation, just because God knew we would need forgiveness.

Jesus didn't need to learn to live as a human; after all, He created everything in man, but He knew we wouldn't know this if He didn't become as we are.

Where else but to Jesus can I go for truth? Where to go for comfort in my suffering, for strength when I am weak? Where but to God who, even after Jesus appeared on earth, was crucified, and arose from the grave and who in this great mystery, knew we needed Him so much He sent His Holy Spirit to live in our heart and minds.

Oh, what a wonderful mystery.

Just as the scripture tells us, "Mary the mother of Jesus, pondered these things in her heart." So do I.

In 1929, C. Bishop wrote the Hymn "Such Love." Can you comprehend how God could love sinners such as us? Yet He did, so as the song says, we can sing "Such love, such wondrous love / how wonderful is love like this!"

For God so loved the people of the world; He gave His Son that we might receive eternal life.

PACKING

Packing, even the word can be exciting or just another name for work.

It's pretty clear when you start packing, what we wanted yesterday, we don't want to today, so out goes those items we "just had to have."

When moving into a different house, we often need to get rid of a lot we brought into our old house. The furniture may be wrong, and it just won't do. So out it goes. There is plenty of evidence all around—thrift stores, garage sales—all proclaiming "I don't want these things anymore."

This is the way it is when we turn our lives over to God. We look at the things in our life, and they don't look right. And they sure don't fit into our new life in Jesus.

But the most wonderful news is we don't have to go out and search for new items. Jesus said He will give us all we need, His peace, His Joy that He has already paid for with His own blood on the cross.

We are reminded in the Bible, these gifts never grow old, but they are renewed every morning.

LIFE CHANGES

In the military, there are many different ranks, from generals to the privates. During war, some are on the front line taking bullets, digging trenches, and pursuing into the enemy line.

There are chaplains who bring encouragement and strength.

But sometimes overlooked is the medical unit that is always present where the battle is.

They are so vital they go even before the battle starts, preparing because they know there will be wounded. They know their care is needed so the soldiers will be capable of fighting again.

All of these soldiers are needed—those on the front line, those who give the orders, and those who follow the orders. Especially needed are the unseen who give physical and spiritual help during the battle.

So are we, as Christians in a war, a spiritual war. Some are called to be on the front line that is seen, but then there are the unseen, but all are part of God's army.

As our season in life changes, we may no longer be seen, but we are still vital, binding up the wounds, helping the battle weary.

No matter how we are serving God, we are God's army.

THE HOUSE

It was an exciting day when the plans were certified stamped and ready to be built.

After going over each detail with the general contractor, and the price was agreed, the contract was signed, and the work was ready to begin.

At first, all that was seen was a big hole in the ground, until the foundation was laid. Soon, hammering and sawing could be heard as slowly the walls were stood up. Next the roof was covered, and now it looked like soon there would be a house.

The general called in his subcontractor to put in the rough electrical and plumbing. Now envisioning became easier. It was exciting when the next contractor came in, and with great artistic ability, a stone fireplace dominated the room. Much was left to do, but the contractor, at the right time, called in others to Sheetrock, paint and, at the very last, lay my beautiful carpet.

It was still pretty chilly visiting until a new man showed up, and soon heat was coming out of the registers.

Back came the electricians and plumbers, and there stood the sinks and tubs.

It took many different people with different skills to erect the house that would become my home.

Jesus said He is building His house, His church. He is the great Architect and the general Contractor, and He paid the price, but we are His people that He has given different talents to build His church.

Aren't you thankful no matter how small your part, we are all working together with the same purpose, building God's house, His church made up of all true believers from the ends of this earth?

As we all work together, we have God's promise that even the gates of hell can't overcome His church.

POPCORN AND MOVIES

I am blessed to have children. My daughter and son-in-law, who in every sense is my son, purchased a home with a cozy mother-in-law apartment and encouraged me to spend the winter out of the Montana snow.

While Gary would be exercising, Penny and I would curl up in our robes with a Coke and a bowl of popcorn covered in butter. We both love old classic movies, with *Pride and Prejudice* being a favorite.

The author, Jane Austin, started writing her novel in 1797, and it was published in 1813. Since then, there has been at least six different versions.

The story line is based on the English countryside with, of course, the rich man and a mother wanting her daughter to marry.

The other day, I was thinking about *Pride and Prejudice* and how it affects all of us.

Pride is an inside attitude that Scripture tells us God hates. So what is pride? Is it not being proud of a job well done, until the enemy of our soul creeps in, and we forget how God has given us the ability and resources to do what we do and then we get all puffed up and look around, thinking we are somewhat better than someone else?

Prejudice is more than looking at the color of someone's skin or so-called status in life. It is really just *prejudging* someone.

Yes, it is easy to fall to pride and prejudice. It is a tool of the enemy that steeps in to corrupt our heart.

There are many different versions of *pride* and *prejudice*, just as there are many people.

We must guard our hearts and minds from ever thinking we are better than anyone else. We need to humble ourselves before God and confess our own hidden pride, arrogance, and prejudice.

And thanks to our forgiving Father, He will cleanse us from this sin.

SARAH

Sarah Lockwood Pardee was born around 1839 into a rich upper-class family. By the age of twelve, she spoke four languages. With all her privileges, she attended the Yale school for girls. She became known as the Belle of New Haven.

As part of high society, she was married in 1862 to William Winchester. Their only child, a daughter, died at one month old. Her father-in-law died, and then her husband in 1881 from tuberculosis. At his death, she inherited millions and 50 percent holdings of Winchester Repeating Arms Company.

Sarah had a brilliant mind but held to the belief of the occult teaching of the Rosicrucians that taught there is secret wisdom and human enlighten.

Some accounts say after her husband died, she traveled to foreign countries for three years. But what is known is after his death, she consulted a medium who told her that the spirits of the dead killed in the civil war with the Winchester rifle were trying to kill her, so the only way to appease them was to build them a house.

She moved to California, living close to her sister, where she bought an unfinished farmhouse on 162 acres and continued her life in high society. She was called eccentric.

Still plagued by fear for thirty-eight years, she never stopped building on her house for the dead. She had no architect but herself. She built a séance room where she would go into for plans of what to build next. She tried to trick the spirits by building stairs to nowhere, doors to nowhere, and cupboards some just one inch deep. The house grew to seven stories high and rooms were discovered after her death in 1922. The cost was millions, and it was sold to investors who turned it into a museum.

You can see the evidence of her tortured soul when you visit what is called the Winchester Mystery House in California.

To us as believers, Sarah was not eccentric but a lost soul, and so are those among us today who say all roads lead to God.

Don't you wonder who or what started them down a road that goes nowhere? Do you think maybe it is because we don't tell them who Jesus is, God in human flesh, and they can't bypass God to get to God?

Maybe if we show them the right road to the only true God and our Savior Jesus, then they will know the truth that will set them free.

WHY

There is no accident with God. What He plans and purposes will happen.

And that is why you are here. He formed you in your mother's womb. And now as a believer, you are born again.

The answer of why is simply because He loves you.

God's way is not our way because we do not understand as God knows. But our responsibility is important enough that God gave us life physically and spiritually.

God can't use us as He wants until we surrender our will to His. This is not a onetime surrender but each day and sometimes a struggle of faith.

If, as Scripture tells, I am to live one day at a time, then we are supposed to listen for His voice in our spirit.

Jesus said, "I speak to my sheep and they know my voice."

So relax, seek, rest; you are where you are supposed to be, being prepared for the next new assignment.

Just know this, it's not just in doing but in the being that God desires of us. We are to live for God's glory, but how do you bring glory to God? Simply by giving the credit to God; after all, everything we have He has given to us. Why does God who does not need glory want us to give Him the glory?

It is simple. So people will turn to Him, following Him, not you because He loves you and the person you are helping. He knows they need Him more than they need you, and when they turn to Him, you have fulfilled a part of His plan and the purpose God has for you.

Isn't that exciting to think about!

THE SOURCE OF MUSIC

Is anyone among you in trouble? Let them pray.
Is anyone happy? Let them sing songs of praise.
—James 5:13

It is amazing you can sing and praise God in both circumstances, troubled or happy.

Bill and Glory Gaither, well-known gospel singers and writers, told us why in a song they wrote. I don't know if it was in trouble or if they were happy, but they told us it was because God gave the song.

Read these words and sing.

You ask me why my heart keeps singing, why I can sing when things go wrong, but since I've found the source of music, I just can't help it God gave the song.

The third verse says day after day that song goes on for once you know the source of music you'll always hear it God gave the song.

In our life experiences as we trust in God in trouble or happy, let God give you the song and just as the Gaithers wrote, "But since I've found the source of music I just can't help it."

God gave the song.

You can listen to the song "God Gave the Song" on the internet.

UNSEEN

It was unseen and carried around by people unaware of it. They affected others they came in contact with.

Where was their hope?

They tried so hard to defeat this unseen enemy. They treated the symptoms, but it continued to spread.

The experts were called in, and advice was given; some followed, but no relief came.

I'm not speaking of the COVID-19 virus but sin. This virus came from an original virus, just as sin also came from an original sin. We are all born with it. It didn't start in China by an accident but in a garden on purpose when Adam and Eve disobeyed God.

But I have wonderful news.

Jesus died for all mankind that when we believe in *Him*, our original sin can be controlled, not by the washing of our hands and social distancing but by Jesus's blood shed on the cross.

As we pray for a vaccine for COVID-19 to stop the spread of this unseen enemy, we must pray more diligently for the many that don't yet realize we have an unseen enemy, Satan.

Spread the good news that our enemy was defeated over two thousand years ago.

No more social distancing. The closer we are to our Savior and each other, the greater the victory.

THE TITLE

It started in 2016 when Donald J. Trump announced his bid for the presidency of the United States. It continued into 2019 when his opponents tried to impeach him.

Charges were brought through the years; some true and some untrue were hurled about. What was it that aroused his opponents?

It wasn't Donald Trump! It was his title, the president of the United States, because they knew without the title, he had no power.

He didn't give the title to himself, but it was given by the people.

We all have an opponent who started against us when we first started seeking a title, one that no one but the Almighty God could bestow on us.

First, this opponent charged us with things that were true but also things untrue (like God can't love you).

But God's truth is stronger than our opponent, Satan.

No president can keep his title for more than eight years. But as the redeemed children of God, we have been given our title for eternity, and just as the president has no power without his title, neither do we.

Just as Donald Trump's opponents have not given up, neither will our opponent. But we have the very words of God's promise found in Romans 8:38–39,

> For I am convinced that neither death nor life, neither angels nor demons, neither the present nor the future nor any powers, neither height nor depth, nor anything else in all creation, will be able to separate us from the love of God that is in Christ Jesus our Lord.

FREEDOM

Darkness was so deep it covered the land, and fear fell upon the people.

Just as the dark of night comes after the light and the dusk of evening, so this darkness came.

There had been wars before the people had been united, but now a deep divide was among the young nation. Of the thirty-five states, fifteen had rebelled, and eleven had elected their own president, Jefferson Davis, and were threatening to secede from the Union. Jefferson, a southerner, was a known man, a former senator and secretary of war.

The cancer of sin ran deep. Yes, many had spoken out against the injustice of slavery. Two Quaker brothers, the Op den Graeffs, and others who were of the thirteen families which founded William Penn's land, signed the first petition against slavery in 1688. A brave woman, Harriet Beecher Stowe, wrote a book in 1852 based on facts and truth of slavery that became known as *Uncle Tom's Cabin*. This truth helped wake up others to what was going on. Many, known only to God, formed what is now known as the Underground Railroad that helped some of the millions of slaves escape the horror and degradation they were subject to at the hands of greedy land owners…and others brave in heart spoke out.

Then a man so conscience stricken and morally opposed could not tolerate this cancer so, in 1854, started speaking out. When he, Abraham Lincoln, became our sixteenth president, he issued the Emancipation Proclamation in 1861, freeing the slaves.

The law was passed, but it did not bring freedom!

War broke out, state against state, family against family, and brother against brother.

For four years the battles were fought and over six hundred thousand men died and homes were destroyed. There were thousands of Black soldiers who died to free men from slavery most of the soldiers from the free northern states and fighting with the Union Army who fought the Confederate Army. When this great war was being fought, it was to free almost 3.5 million slaves, one-third of the population of the confederate states.

The war ended. Robert E. Lee, the Confederate Army leader, surrendered to Ulysses Grant of the Union Army on April 9, 1865.

Abraham Lincoln was assassinated by a southern sympathizer just days later on April 15, 1865.

The law was passed, but it did not bring freedom for all. Some lived under oppression and some because they did not understand their freedom

Yes, law was passed, but it did not bring freedom!

One hundred ten years later, in 1955, another great man, Martin Luther King Jr., a minister who knew no man is superior to another, just equal, began speaking out against the injustice in some states.

He did not want violence but was an advocate of justice by peaceful demonstration. His famous speech "I Have a Dream" is known by many. It was his call and of many of his followers.

It is said he wanted his speech to be like Abraham Lincoln's in the Gettysburg Address.

On April 28, 1963, this great man was speaking at the Lincoln Memorial and called Lincoln a great man. Now another great man was speaking out from his heart. "When all men black and white will be free at last" is a phrase from an old Negro spiritual: "Free at last / at last, Great God, we are free at last."

And once again, a great man, Martin Luther King Jr., was assassinated on April 4, 1968. Yes, again laws were passed, but they did not bring freedom to the hearts.

Where there are wounds, there are scars.

We wonder how could we see the evil of slavery and do nothing? How could we see the horror of the Holocaust and do nothing?

How can we know of the murder of babies being aborted now and do nothing?

Compliancy—dull hearts that shut out the very word of God. "What you do to these the least you do unto me."

Laws are passed, but it does not bring freedom of the heart!

Until we understand the depravity of sin, we can't understand the love of God that sets all men free from the slavery of sin.

Then we can be, as Martin Luther Jr. said, "free at last," not by law but by the love of God, the love that sets our hearts free to love one another as the Holy Father, the Son, and the Holy Spirit who loves us all.

Yes, laws can be passed, but it is love that sets us free!

Free at last!

WHO IS LEADING?

God led His people from the slavery in Egypt to the Promised Land, providing all their needs. His presence went with them in a cloud and fire.

So is God leading us from the slavery of sin to the Promised Land, and just as he guided them, the Holy Spirit is leading us, providing us all we need.

His manna from heaven nourished their bodies, and His word nourishes us.

Their journey was hard because of their rebellion and from forces outside their control, just as our life journey can be hard when we rebel against our Lord or from forces outside our ability to change.

Like the Israelites, we too have God's promise of a better home.

You see, as Solomon said, "There is nothing new under the sun." But there is a *Son* over all, and His Spirit goes before us to lead us home.

There is a wonderful song written by E. W. Blandly in 1890 with the words "I will follow where He leads me / no turning back / no turning back."

One Salvation Army officer, when he was called to the slums in New York's waterfront, has been quoted as saying, "He will give me grace and glory. I'll go with him all the way."

As believers, that should be our testimony because we know He will be with us all the way.

No turning back, no turning back!

SOWING SEEDS

In Mark 4, Jesus told a parable of a farmer who went out to sow his seed. Some fell along the path, and the birds came and ate it. Some fell on rocky places where it didn't have much soil. It sprang up quickly, but because the soil was shallow, when the sun came up, it withered because it had no root. Some of the seed fell among the thorns that choked the seed out, so it didn't mature into fruit. Still there were some seed that fell on good soil. It grew and produced a good crop.

Jesus asked his disciples, "Do you understand what I have said?" and then explained. The farmer is one sowing God's word.

Some people are like the seed along the path. As soon as they hear God's word, Satan comes and takes what was sown *in* them away.

Some hear with great joy, receive it, but since they have no root, they last only a short time. When trouble comes because of their belief in God, they quickly fall away.

Some hear, but like the thorns, the worries of life, deceitfulness of wealth, and the desire for other things choke out God's word, and they don't produce fruit.

Still other seed were sown in good soil. The word was heard, people accepted the truth, and matured into a crop.

In all the people, the seed / God's word was sown in them.

As I understand what Jesus said, I realize I have been all the different people at one time in my life. But all praise to God, His faithful farmers just kept sowing seed, His truth, until they took root, grew, and produced faith.

Like the parable in John 15, Jesus tells us He is the Vine, and we are the branches. And eleven times He tells us to remain in Him, and if we remain, we will produce the fruit of the Holy Spirit.

Just as the farmer in the parable didn't stop, so must we keep on sowing God's truth. We might not know what will result, but as God said, "My word will not come back void."

SHORTCUTS

Even if you don't like where you are in your life, it is still your life, made of the choices you have made and some choices others have made that has affected your life. Our past is a part of today but also tomorrow.

Everything in our life as a Christian is preparing us and is teaching us how to live God's plan for us. When we are ready, in God's perfect timing and as we seek God, we can gain a deeper insight in some of our trials, *but* not all until we get home.

Jesus said, "Seek and you will find." Yes, everything in a believer's life is allowed, but only and not more than we can bear when God is with us.

So don't ignore your trial. It is a reality, but trust the very one who saved you for life everlasting. He is your strength. Mourning and grieving are much deeper than sorrow, and God knows our weakness.

God knows all our secrets, and yet still loves us in spite of our sins. He will forgive and, even still, use us as we submit to the perfect plan He had for us before we were born.

There are no shortcuts in this life, and we must all go through many kinds of trials, but His word gives us hope.

As we go through the trial, waiting and wondering can be heartbreaking. His promise is He hears our cries. He sees our pain, but God knows the big picture. Keep going. God is doing something, developing in us what only waiting can do.

In the early 1900s, there was a young preacher and carpenter, George Young. He lived on a meager salary but managed to build a home for his family. One day while he was away preaching in a different area, some evil men came and burnt his home to the ground.

It was out of this great trial he wrote a beloved hymn, "God Leads His Dear Children Along."

This is his testimony in the words of his song:

In shady green pastures so rich and so sweet
God leads his dear children along
Where the water's cool flow bathes the weary
    one's feet.
Sometimes on the mountain where the sun
    shines bright
Sometimes in the valley, in darkness of night
Though sorrows befall us and Satan oppose
Through grace we can conquer, defeat all our
    foes.

Then he concludes:

Some through the waters, some through the flood
Some through the fire but all through the blood
Some through great sorrow but God gives a song
In the night season and all the day long.

Yes, George Young knew by experience every word, from the floods to the fire of his home, but his faith was in God that gave him this song written in 1903.

CALENDARS

As a believer, we are told to seek knowledge, understanding, and discernment.

So as we pray, we need to know true prayer is a conversation with God, not just a lot of words spoken without honesty. Because our prayer is not in the past or future, we need to talk to God about today.

As we read the very words of God, if we are sincere, we must ask, "What is God saying to me?"

Our daily devotion is just being with God in a quiet setting. It's not the quest of reading so many chapters a day though that is good, but it can become easy to mark that off your religious day planner, like eating your breakfast. You can read all you want, know what it says but not know why. You may have more knowledge but no understanding.

When we sincerely seek God's truth, He said His Holy Spirit gives us understanding and discernment.

We have just one life, and as we seek His wisdom, He reveals His plan for us. Imperfect as we are, if we are in His will, it is perfect in God's eyes even if not in man's.

Our purpose in life is not for tomorrow but now and will be in the future. We don't get through the day to enjoy tomorrow, but we are to live this day in His presence.

So enjoy your quiet time with the one who loves you with a love beyond understanding. Listen to that quiet voice of the Holy Spirit as he leads you into God's wisdom, and as He promised, you will live this day knowing He is our strength, our peace, and our joy.

TWO BROTHERS

Do you need a lesson on forgiveness? Do you think no one could understand just how much you have been hurt by those who should have loved and protected you? Did someone cause you great financial harm?

There is someone who could have told you they understand and know how you feel.

Many years ago in a culture much different from ours, twins were born. One loved hunting and the outdoors; the other stayed close to home. In too many cases, their parents chose favorites.

The older brother was to inherit the greater amount financially (as was the custom) and lead the next generation. That was what was supposed to be, but that is not what happened.

The brothers grew to manhood, and as they grew, they also grew apart.

Through carelessness, the older gave away his right as the firstborn to his younger brother. That was his choice, but what happened later was what was unforgivable.

Through deceit and dishonesty, his younger brother, with the help of their mother, stole his father's blessing and the right to lead the family.

His hatred was deep, and he was making plans to kill his brother, but not yet. Hate runs deep and festers, so waiting for the right time consumed everything he did.

In fear, the younger brother fled the country.

Twenty years passed, and the great deceiver we know as Jacob was returning to his home country. He had learned what deceit was. He had deceived his brother once, but he had been deceived eleven times. Now a changed man with a new name, Israel, he was filled with regret and guilt. Fear, deep consuming fear, was his companion. He knew his brother Esau was near, and he remembered his murderous threat.

The time came when the brothers met on the road. What was on the brothers' hearts? Repentance for Jacob, and can you imagine Esau had already forgiven his brother, the very one who had stolen his destiny?

Genesis 25:23 through Genesis 33 tells us just how much was forgiven and what can happen when we do.

Now what is it you can't forgive?

I WILL

I am confident in God's love for me. Only God can help me in my deepest need. You, God, sees me. You, God, hears me. You, God, understands me.

For this reason,

- I will trust your strength when I am weak.
- I will seek your wisdom when I don't know what to do.
- I will believe every promise you have given before they happen.
- I will remember what you have already done for me.
- I will remember this too is only temporal.
- I will remember I am not alone. You are always with me.

When I forget this, and I will, I will trust your Holy Spirit to rekindle this fire in me and renew me until once again, I will.

HOME

His father was a prosperous man, so he stayed home and settled on the farm. Each morning as the sun rose, he would get up early, feed the animals, then go into the fields to plant seeds for the coming harvest.

That is what people saw, but what was really happening?

As the sun rose, he would rise early, care for the animals, then go to the fields and plant seeds. What seeds? Resentment, anger, jealousy. Why? It was his brother's fault! Just as Cain resented Abel and killed him, so he resented his brother too.

As he harbored the seeds (thoughts) about his brother partying and being with prostitutes, having a great time, he was working this stinking farm.

Makes you wonder how he knew what his brother was doing. Maybe that is what he wanted to do too.

That is what he was thinking, but what was happening?

The day came when his brother came home. The life he had been living had broken his health and his spirit. His only hope was his father's compassion.

One brother left, and one brother stayed home; both were prodigals. One was visible, the other masked in hypocrisy and deceit.

There may be times in our lives when we are like both brothers. One left our Father but returned; one stayed but not in spirit. Both were loved by the Father, just as we are. The Father met one and rejoiced at his return, and the Father left his house and went to his other son, told him of his love and begged him to come home too.

That is our Father. All of us are loved, and all are welcomed home no matter which prodigal we are.

ALL WRAPPED UP

It's that time of the year; the lights are flickering, and the bulbs are carefully hung from the branches. The tree stands in its place of honor.

Our hearts are lifted as we gaze at the beauty of the tree and hear the music that is played again this season of the year.

But what do we wait for? It's what is under the tree.

I have always admired those who have the artistic ability to wrap those packages that are so appealing, but it brings back memories of when my daughter and son-in-law were poor. They had sacrificed for what was inside the brown-paper wrapping.

It reminds me no matter the outside, it's what is inside that counts. The Bible tells us, "Man looks on the outside but God looks inside."

So let's not judge by someone's outside beauty or lack thereof. It is what is inside that counts.

IT'S ALL ABOUT ME!

Jesus said, "Love others."

Starts with me; thought you'd like that. You see, it is all about me loving you.

How? Like God loves me.

"Impossible," you say, "That's not natural." Right, it's from God.

So since it's about God loving me, I am supposed to love you.

How does God love me? Remember this is about me. Am I perfect? Do I sin? Do I hurt others? Do I sin—yes, sin. But God still loves me. Did God forgive me? Yes, He does and loves me, and He shows me mercy when I don't deserve it, time after time.

So you see, it is all about me loving you. It's not a perfect love story with a fairytale ending, but it's the story of perfect love, God's love for you and me.

Now let's see how I love you. Yes, I remember it is like God loves me, this imperfect being that still makes a mess of things and needs a lot of forgiving and loving.

When I remember that, it makes it easier for me to love you. It becomes easier to not be me and you but us.

FRUIT

The fruit of the Spirit only becomes evident in our lives as we learn and grow in the Holy Spirit.

As we die daily to our will and live as the Holy Spirit leads, so will His fruit become evident in our lives. His peace, joy, and contentment will become ours.

We must grow in the Spirit. Jesus said, "I am the vine, you are the branches." It is the vine that produces the fruit that matures. So it is in our lives. The Holy Spirit produces the fruit in our lives.

Just as it takes time for fruit to mature, so it is that the fruit of the Holy Spirit in our lives takes time.

The Holy Spirit is God's gift to us. It is the Holy Spirit that leads us to salvation; it is the Holy Spirit that teaches us in God's truth. The Holy Spirit leads and guides us, and it is His strength that overcomes our weakness.

"The fruit of the Spirit is love, joy, peace, patience, kindness, goodness, faithfulness, gentleness and self-control" (Galatians 5:22).

Only as we live as the Holy Spirit leads will we begin to produce His fruit in our lives.

Just as it takes fruit in our garden time to mature, so it does in our lives. Just as God has provided all that is needed for our gardens to mature, so the Holy Spirit has given us all we need to grow in the Spirit.

The fruit is always the Spirit's; we only reflect it as we live in His truth.

NEWBORN

Why is it that we want to see that newborn baby? After all, if we admit it, most of them aren't much to look at. They are red, wrinkled, and with no teeth or hair.

But we are in awe at the new life.

That's the way we were when we were born again. None of us was much to look at either.

But just as the mother sees past all the imperfections, so our Lord sees the beauty in a born-again life.

He knows we will grow and will learn to walk and talk just as the newborn will.

Jesus said we are to become as a child, knowing we are helpless, and nothing we can do can save us. Just as the baby did nothing for new life, we need in humility to accept the free gift of life by believing what John 3:16 says. "For God so loved the world that He gave His only son that whoever believes in Him will have eternal life."

Thanks be to Jesus for the free gift, and as we learn to walk in His ways, even when we stumble and fall, He picks us up, encourages us, and we will grow in the wonderful plans He has for us.

Life is wonderful; rejoice in the love of God.

WHO CARES?

There are many times in our life when we try to explain our troubles to someone who can't understand, but God sees our tears and our broken hearts and life.

Jesus/God fully understands. He, like us, had a body of flesh and bones when He lived and walked here on earth.

He knows what it is like to be hungry and tired. He felt loneliness when His disciples deserted Him during the agony of His trial and crucifixion.

He was heartbroken when His father died and His brothers did not believe him. His body felt excruciating pain at the cross.

We know He loved others and cried when His friend died.

He showed mercy when a woman caught in adultery was dragged before Him. He saw the injustice that the man was not there too.

He was tempted just as we are but did not sin.

He saw the political upheaval and the hypocrisy of the religious leaders. He cared then, and He cares now!

He sees our tears, and when no one understands, He does; he cried too.

This all-powerful Ruler is our friend who understands. He says in Philippians 4:7, His peace (He is peace) will guard our heart and mind.

"Let us fix our eyes on Jesus, the author and perfecter of our faith, who for joy set before Him endured the cross" (Hebrews 12:2).

So remember who cares, who sees those tears when your heart is broken. He knows. He felt that way too, Jesus our Savior.

ARE YOU LISTENING?

When the Holy Spirit disciplines us, He is training us.

When we aren't convicted and don't feel our need to admit our sin (because that is what it is), we grieve the Holy Spirit, and we will not change.

It is wonderful to know when the Holy Spirit speaks to us. It is proof we are His sheep.

Jesus said, "My sheep know my voice." His kind and loving voice speaks to each of us, and as we learn to hear His voice and follow with obedience, joy and peace are ours.

What a privilege that the Almighty, powerful Ruler of heaven and earth speaks to us. So be listening as John 10:27 says, "My sheep listen to me."

So when that still small voice speaks to you, be thankful and know you are His.

IDOLS

They had already run him out of two towns. What had he done?

Upon entering a new town, he was waiting for friends to join him. As he waited, he toured the town, and as he did, he was greatly distressed at what he saw. The beautiful city of Athens was full of idols. What he did next is what he always did. He went to the local synagogue to reason with the Jews who lived there. Day after day, wherever he went and whoever would listen, he would speak to them.

One day, a group of men, Epicureans and Stoic philosophers began to disagree with him, so they invited him to come up to Mars Hill, 370 feet above the city, to explain to them what he was talking about.

Paul now started to speak with them. "I see you are quite religious you even have an idol to an unknown god." So Paul told them, "What is an unknown to you, I am going to tell you." As he told them of the one and only true God, some laughed, and some believed.

You see, these philosophers of Athens spent their time just talking about and listening to new ideas. The Epicureans, followers of Epicurus, believed the sole purpose of man was to achieve happiness in mental, intellectual pursuit and sensual pleasures. The Stoic followers of Zeno taught the universe and nature is god.

As you can see, these teachings are present today.

My question is, do we sometimes have an idol too? Oh, we wouldn't bow down to it, but does someone or something become more important than God?

Would we be willing to be as Apostle Paul, boldly taking our stand as he did, even to being tossed out of our group of friends or ran out of town?

But remember, in each place, in every town, the Bible says "some believed." And to Paul, that was worth it all.

WHEN NOTHING CHANGES

The scriptures tell us God has placed all things under the authority of Jesus. All power in heaven and earth is His.

There are many things that have come or will come into our lives that we can't control and Jesus will not remove. But this we know, the Lord knows all things from the beginning to the end. He has promised all things will work together for our good as we love and trust Him. We also have His great promise, "I withhold nothing good from those who believe."

In 1887, John Sammis wrote the hymn "Trust and Obey," one of the best-loved hymns that is sang in many churches today.

One verse says "Not a burden we bear / not a sorrow we share / but our toil He doth richly repay / Not a grief or a loss / not a frown or a care / but is blest if we trust and obey / for there's no other way / to be happy in Jesus / but to trust and obey."

So when nothing changes, and we are discouraged, just remember God's promises and trust and obey.

MEASURING

There are many ways to gauge if things are as they should be.

It's important to have the air in your tires equal and have the right pressure, so a gauge is used to check them.

Basements and enclosed areas can have too much humidity with the result of mold, so there is a meter to show what the comfort level is. There are inside and outside thermometers.

There are many ways the health system use as gauges to determine the status of our body.

But there is one all-important gauge. It's how much we love God. You can find the gauge in 1 John 5:1–2. "This is love for God, to obey His commands, and His commands are not burdensome."

Very simple. Our obedience to God's word shows us how much we love Him.

"And this is love that we walk in obedience to His commands" (2 John 1:6).

Aren't you glad you don't have to wonder how much we love God? All we have to do is look at our obedience that according to Scripture is an accurate measure of our love.

WHAT CAN WE KNOW?

Marilyn was her name.

Her fragile body couldn't hide the twinkle in her brown eyes.

As she sat in her wheelchair, she began to speak. The ladies around her listened, not just with their ears but with their hearts.

Marilyn leaned forward as she told us her story. Marilyn grew up in the years of Martin Luther King, part of an only Black family in an all-White community.

She told of her experiences, the loneliness and broken relationships. But she also spoke about the love of her family.

As she was concluding, she said, "First we were called Negroes, then colored, now Black." Then she chuckled. "I don't even know what I'm supposed to call myself." Then with the sweetest smile added, "But I know who I am, a child of God."

What a lesson we learned that day. We are not what others call us—Black, White, rich, or poor. It's not where we came from; it is whose we are and where we are going.

And just like Marilyn, we can know whose we are because of the cross of Jesus.

WHAT'S AGE GOT TO DO WITH IT?

By my chronological and spiritual age, I have learned a lot of what I need to know, and what I don't yet know, God is still teaching me.

What a wonderful Savior.

So on our journey of life, we need to keep all our problems in perspective and know He is with us. His Holy Spirit will guide and direct us. And best of all, we have a map, God's words written down for all to see.

Enjoy the little things. They are God's blessings. So much we take for granted until they aren't there anymore.

There was a part-time preacher who preached at various churches. He was not considered a great preacher but faithful, and he always wanted a deeper spiritual life.

His name was Johnson Oatman Jr. Thinking of what he already had, in 1897, he wrote the song "Count Your Blessings." The words "name them one by one, and you will be surprised what the Lord has done" is the theme of the song.

God used this faithful man as He also wrote the hymns "Higher Ground" and "No Not One."

He may not have been considered a great preacher of his time, but because of his longing to grow in the faith, God is still speaking through his songs 120 years later.

No matter our age, spiritual or chronological, we still have a lot of growing.

What a journey we are all on, and what an abundant life when we learn to "count our many blessings."

And yes, it does surprise us what the Lord has already done.

ALIGNMENT

Living in snow country each year, it is important to have your tires changed to keep you safe.

Loading up my winter snow tires, I went to town to keep my appointment.

I knew I had time, so after getting a bag of popcorn, I sat down to wait until they made the change from my summer tires.

It wasn't long before a man came to me and said my tires that they were changing had some damage, so if they put on my new tires, they would be damaged too unless they did an alignment on my car.

I don't understand how such things work, but I trusted they knew. You see, I had been going there for years and trusted them. So the alignment was done. And my new tires would be free from sustaining damage.

Our spiritual lives can get out of alignment too. We might encounter something on our journey through this life that will cause damage, unless we align our life with God. After all, haven't we been going to Him all these years, and yes, don't we trust Him to do just what we need?

SKYDIVING

You have seen them, those heroes of the sky that aren't afraid of falling.

No, they just jump and glide through the air. Well, I'm not about to be one of them.

But wait! Yes, I am one. You see, I am an early riser, my favorite time of the day. I need no alarm to wake up in the early hours of the morning while it is still dark.

With coffee in hand just before daybreak, God greets me with an array of beautiful colors—reds, orange, and yellows—all announcing His sun is rising over the mountain. Soon the dark is replaced with a brilliant light. I can't look up now because the light blinds me, but now I can see all around clearer.

When darkness returns, it is not because of the absence of the sun. We just can't see it, but the moon that has no light is reflecting the sun. Soon the stars will be spread across this vast universe, all proclaiming God's message to us.

God sent His Son to be with us. He promised He would never leave us or forsake us. Just as He is with us in the dark of our circumstances, we only need to look up. He is there, and when the morning comes, we will see more clearly.

So you see, I am a skydiver.

EACH DAY

Life in this world seems more uncertain every day. But Jesus said, "I am with you. Do not fear. I am your strength." Do we believe that? Then live each day like we do.

In 1918, James Wells wrote the song "Living by Faith."

> I care not today what tomorrow may bring
> If shadow or sunshine or rain
> The Lord I know ruleth over everything
> And all of my worries are vain.
>
> The tempest may flow and the storm clouds arise
> Obscuring the brightness of life,
> I'm never alarmed at the overcast skies;
> The Master looks on at the strife.
>
> I know that He safely will carry me through
> No matter what evils betide.
> Why should I then care that the tempest may
>   blow
> If Jesus walks close to my side?
>
> Living by faith in Jesus above,
> Trusting, confiding in His great love
> Safe from all harm in His sheltering arm
> I'm living by faith and feel no alarm.

James Wells had a friend R. E. Winsett. After reading his song, he wrote the last verse:

> Our Lord will return to this earth some sweet day
> Our troubles then will be o'er.
> The Master so gently will lead us away
> Beyond that blest heavenly shore.

One wrote how to live by faith, and one wrote why. Jesus will return to this earth, and then all the trouble will be over.

Oh, yes, and J. L. Heath wrote the music. So until then, live by faith safe in His love (2 Corinthians 5:17).

COMMITMENT

What would you say about a man that after sixty years, never brought his wife flowers, and through the years, no jewelry, not even on their fiftieth anniversary?

I don't even have to guess because I know what you would think. The nicest thing you are thinking is "What a jerk!"

Now let me tell you what kind of man who did such a thing.

- A man that loved his family, one that was there every night. One that brought his paycheck home and never said the money is mine; I earned it.
- A man that when he saw someone needed a suit or set of tires, gave them the resources to pay for them.
- A man that left notes written on scraps of paper in his lunch box, thanking his wife for his lunch. A man that left the note "to the Winchester widow" when he left for his hunting trip.
- A man that thought cards and flowers were a waste of money but bragged to everyone about his wife's flower gardens.
- A man who stayed in his wife's hospital room for a month when she had cancer surgery, who knew she loved lambs and brought her a reindeer because it was December, and he couldn't find a lamb.
- A man that came running into the room when he found on the beach in Mexico a little license plate with the year 1958, the year of their marriage.

- Fifty years later, a man that as he was confined to a nursing home the last year of his life, would say to his nurse, "I love Georgia, and no one is going to come between us."
- A man that prayed for his family and loved his God.

That is the man that never gave his wife flowers.

We can learn a lesson from such a man. We are to let nothing come before our love for God and love others as we want to be loved.

Flowers fade, jewelry loses its luster, but he was a man that knows what true love is. He didn't give things; he gave himself.

BEAVERS

Growing up in the 1940s on a farm with a river on two sides, there was a source of beavers. Here the traps would be set, and the beaver would end up stretched out on a board. Now you wonder why anyone would want to trap a beaver.

First, they were a source of income. Their pelts would be sold for they had soft underfur that was used for hats and coats. And yes, they provided healthy meat to eat.

The beavers are very intelligent and have great skill in building their houses in streams that can be large enough to stop the flow of the rivers and streams. But they can be trapped when something they crave entices them into a trap.

Beavers are just like us.

The Scripture tells us we too can be trapped. The devil doesn't tempt us in our strong areas but in our weakest area…The fur trappers all used the same bait that had a horrible smell to us, but the beaver loved it and were drawn to it.

Scripture warns us we have a trapper out to entice and trap us too, and he, the devil, knows just the bait to use. It is tailor-made for each of us. He used an apple to entice Eve because she saw that it was good for knowledge. David was enticed when he lusted after Bathsheba, Achan when he craved silver and gold, but the biggest deception of all was on the religious leaders that crucified Jesus because they loved their power.

Yes, Satan deceives with a trap just for us.

But praise is to Jesus. Unlike the beaver, if we fall into the devil's trap, we can defeat the one who has come to rob us. Jesus provided the way. "If we confess our sin, He is willing to forgive."

But best of all, if we walk in His light, we have the ability to recognize the trap and, by the grace of God, avoid the devil's plan to destroy us.

We are warned, "Be alert." Don't be deceived, but be an overcomer by the power of God who one day is going to destroy the one who comes to us to deceive and destroy.

To God give praise.

AN OLD PROVERB

There is an old proverb that originated in the 1690s during the war between the French and the Iroquois Indians.

The French invited the Iroquois to attend a peace conference and then slaughtered or captured them. Thus the proverb "The white man speaks with a forked tongue," meaning deceptive.

Many today are speaking deception, words that have divided and are deceiving our country, and unless God's church, His believers, wake up, the country will get more and more evil.

In 1 Chronicles 12:32, the Bible tells us there were men of Issachar who understood the times and knew what to do. Israel was a divided war-torn nation at the time, just as ours is today.

God speaks through the generations and tells us what we are to do. "If my people who are called by My name will confess their sin and turn from their wicked ways I will restore their land."

We are not to put our trust in man or government and mighty armies but in God, the Creator of man.

We must learn not to take advice from weak believers or unbelievers. We are to see our sins as God does and know our total dependence is in the Lord. We need a hunger for God's truth and have the boldness to speak His truth in love.

Most of all, remember, don't be silent. Pray that God will save our nation.

Our response to today's culture should be grounded in truth and hope.

ALL-POWERFUL

As I understand more and more who God really is, I don't understand why I ever have a smidgen of a doubt that He will take care of me both spiritually and materially.

It is clear God created everything in the spiritual and material world. Before God, through Jesus, created anything materially, He created the spiritual, all the heavenly beings including all the angels.

Before God created humankind, one-third of the angels were thrown out of heaven because they were deceived by Satan, the evil one.

After this, God created our earth with such great care, providing for all our physical needs. God surrounded us with beauty, from the beauty of the earth to the vast array of the sky. Then he made a beautiful garden where He placed His creation in—Adam and Eve. After a time, evil entered the garden and enticed/deceived them to disobey.

But never think that was a surprise to our great Creator. The Bible says Christ was chosen before the creation of the world to take away the curse that came when Adam and Eve sinned, a promise God gave at the time sin entered our world

Many people lived and died before Jesus, God in human form, came to earth to take away all our sins for all people who believe God's promise.

Now this is a great mystery to me. Satan knew Jesus came to save the world. He was told in the garden. *But* Satan did not know the final details. God used Satan by letting his evil kill Jesus.

If Satan knew all, he would never have wanted Jesus killed because it was through His death on the cross and His resurrection from the dead we are saved.

There are many times God used evil for good. Joseph told his brothers, "You (Satan led) meant it for evil." God used it for good, and a whole Jewish nation grew. Many times God has used the evil of Satan (that He has allowed) to work for good. The people of Israel turned from God and became corrupt, and their evil resulted in being driven out of their land. The Holocaust that was so evil, inspired by Satan to destroy them, resulted in their return to their land. If Satan knew that, do you think he would have enticed them to sin?

We must remember there is no power that is greater than God's. Satan has no power not allowed. Satan's power is limited; his time is limited.

God has all power over all, and He is from eternity.

So now how should I live my life? Live in God's Spirit. He will lead me in His way of righteousness, step by step, day by day, each day living so close we can hear His voice, and never forget, every word in the Bible is His voice speaking.

So listen. Obey, and then we have joy in spite of hardship, peace in spite of conflict, even when we don't understand how we can because of the circumstance.

It was pride that caused Satan to fall, so we must never ever let pride enter into our thoughts.

Our salvation is secure. All hell can't snatch it away, but just remember, don't be deceived. It is only by His strength that we will be victorious. He is in control, the mighty, all-powerful one who created all things including us. And we are His.

What a mystery. His ways are not our ways; it is impossible for us to understand.

But this we know and can understand: He died that we may live, and heaven and earth are under His control.

THE PROMISE

God remembered His promise to His people, Israel, spoken by many prophets. We read in the Old Testament the promise that the Messiah would be born. God revealed how and where the promised Savior would be born. And so it came to pass that Jesus was born. The New Testament tells us how He was born, where he was born, and what was happening around the area where this promise was fulfilled.

He wasn't born into a royal family in a palace but to the poorest and in an unrenowned village to a humble girl, the mystery of the virgin birth and the faithful man, a simple carpenter, who was to raise this holy Child, born for all the people, announced to the least favored in their time, shepherds. Jesus so blessed them by telling us He is the good shepherd.

Why didn't the religious leaders recognize this miracle, just the evil king who tried to kill him?

We celebrate the birth of our Lord on this special day, Christmas, and the victory of our Savior's resurrection on Easter.

This same Jesus that was born in Bethlehem is the same Jesus that lives in the heart of all believers. Now that is something to marvel at.

Mary only knew one thing for sure. She was a virgin. She didn't understand how. She was only told she would have a son and she was to name him Jesus and that He would be called Immanuel (God with us) and that He would save His people from their sins. She pondered all she had been told…Even we now have more information than she had, until Jesus was raised from the grave. Then she understood.

It is so amazing that all the prophets from the beginning, even Abraham, the father of our faith, only knew step-by-step.

God, in these last days, has revealed to us, the most blessed of all generation that have ever lived, the fulfillment of His plan of our salvation And yet we still must walk our journey in our lifetime day by day as the blessed Holy Spirit leads us in the plan He has for our lives.

And we must never forget His promise, "I will return," just as all believers from the beginning have rested in this blessed assurance.

Like Mary, we too must trust and ponder the blessed promise in our hearts!

JEWELRY

The cross is more than jewelry; it is the answer to our Christian life. Just as Jesus was crucified to the world, so we are to die to the things of this world.

His cross made us free from man's religion into a relationship with our Father.

God brought us into this world. He chose our parents, where and when we were born. Now God gives us the opportunity to choose what we are going to do with our lives. The biggest choice we will make is where we are going to spend eternity.

We don't have the choice of when we will die but where we will go when we draw our last breath—heaven or hell.

Jesus said that He came to bring us an abundant life, a life filled with joy in spite of hardship, promises that He will never leave us, and so many more.

So make wise choices today because that choice will affect your tomorrows. Do as Joshua said, "As for me and my house, we will serve the Lord."

And when you make that your choice, you will live in the house of the Lord forever (Joshua 24:14–15).

DO YOU MEAN WHAT YOU SAY?

My grandson was a wrestler in high school.

He didn't have any matches with an opposing team until he had spent hours on the mat wrestling with his own team. When his coach thought he was ready and after carefully weighing, he was allowed to wrestle his opponent of the same weight and experience from another team.

One day while I was visiting, it was a training day. My daughter was late getting supper, and it was time to leave.

My grandson told her, "Mom, we can't be late. Coach said if we were not on time, we can't wrestle."

My daughter said, "I'll talk to him, and then you can."

But my grandson said, "Mom, we have to go. It won't do any good for you to talk to him. Coach said we have to be on time, and he meant it."

And so does God mean what He said when Jesus said, "No one comes to the Father but through me."

Trust God. His word never changes now or forever. What peace we have knowing His promises remain forever. What comfort knowing He is the same yesterday and forever.

COMPANY

Living in the Northwest with its many lakes and forest, summertime brings the call "Company!"

Now throughout the year, guests stop by for dinner, a cup of coffee, and a time for visiting, but company, now that's a different matter. That calls for preparation.

The refrigerator is stocked; after all, meals are a priority. The guest room is dusted, and linens must be fresh. Oh, don't forget the bathroom; after all, they are going to open that closet.

When all preparations are done, we wait in expectation of our time together.

Preparations are so important. The better prepared we are, the more enjoyable is our time together. Scripture tells us Jesus is preparing a home for us, not for just a visit but for all eternity.

Are you prepared for His call for you?

Be ready. Live with great expectation. This might be the day Jesus calls you.

Before Jesus went to the cross, He gave us the promise that He was going to the Father to prepare a place for us, and someday, we too will be with Him in the Father's house.

Check it out, John 14:4–6.

CHOOSE CAREFULLY

As trouble comes on our nation, believers and unbelievers alike are affected. The only difference is we who believe in God have an inner strength because we know the Creator of all has promised He will never leave us and He gives us His peace we can't explain, and nothing can take it away.

As a true believer, even now in our country, there are some that have been singled out by those who want to destroy our faith, but the time is coming when we too, like those that have been faithful, will have to choose to follow Jesus and stand for what we believe.

Tony Evans said, "Our generation respected Christianity even if they didn't believe it. This generation not only rejected Christianity, they hate it. They call our faith hate speech."

Jesus told His followers don't be surprised when trouble comes, but He also told them great is your reward.

Throughout history, believers have had to make their stand, and so must we.

Joshua told Israel, "Choose this day who you will serve. As for me and my house, we will serve the Lord."

Elijah asked the people, "How long will you waver between two opinions? If the Lord is God, follow Him, but if Baal is god, follow him." Elijah suffered for his stand, but later, he was taken up to heaven.

The Bible tells of many heroes of the past (and there are many today) who have taken their stand for truth, and great is their reward.

We can't compromise God's truth; just as only 10 percent poison can kill, so can compromise. Choose as Joshua did, "As for me and my house we will serve the Lord."

AMTRAK

I made the call; my decision had been made. I was going on a trip.

My call was answered by a voice called Julie. Soon I realized Julie asked questions but never let me ask any. But I managed to follow the voice.

Julie first asked what city was I departing from, then asked what my final destination was. Now that was taken care of, Julie asked if I wanted to know the cost and if I wanted to book my trip. So I did. Now I knew the time I was to leave, where I was leaving from, and what my final destination was. But the most important was the name of the train, the Empire Builder.

Can you imagine if I didn't know the right train to get on and where my destination was!

I am forever grateful for Jesus, telling us in John 14:6, "I am the way the truth and the life. No one comes to the Father except through me."

I know the way when I depart from this earth and my final destination. I might not know the time, but Jesus paid my ticket, and He knows my time.

When it is time, I won't be traveling alone. My Savior will be with me, making sure I arrive safe. Until then, I will be getting ready for my trip.

TREASURE MAP

Growing up in the forties on a farm was a life filled with simple blessings. One of the blessings came when our Dad bought an old secondhand player piano. Most of the parts of the player were gone, but it still had a sliding door under the keyboard.

As a child, we explored the farm, finding our treasures, and of course, we made a map where we hid them. The piano was the perfect place to hide our treasure map.

There was a man in the 1600s that knew of a treasure so precious he gave his very life so we could also have this treasure. His name is William Tyndale. At this time, only a clergy with a license could own this treasure. His heart grieved because the ordinary person not only could not own the treasure, nor could they read it in their English language. When Tyndale translated the Bible so we could read it, he was tied to a stake, strangled, and finally set on fire.

How can we as believers neglect reading and studying what Jesus gave His life for and William Tyndale gave his life for just so we have the privilege of reading the very words of God?

What a blessing we receive as we learn of God's great love for each of us, the comfort He gives in our sorrows, the strength when we are weak, and the encouragement as we read what others have lived through and yet remained faithful.

We are told how this earth was formed, how God provided everything just for us, and how He longs for a relationship with each of us right where we are.

If we want all God has for us, we must seek Him. We must learn not just how to feel good but how to be good.

There is a reason God has His very words written for us. It is not to just sit on our table or carry to church, but we are to read it, meditate on it, obey it. It is our very life.

So treasure your gift, God's very words. If you wonder if God is speaking to you, remember He is speaking to you in every word you are reading.

What a treasure we own.

THE WORST JOB

There was a TV program that was based on the worst jobs, but none compares to the job Obadiah had.

From the outside, you would have envied him; you would have seen his position and benefits. So what was his job?

He was in charge of a king's palace. Sounds wonderful if you didn't know the truth.

The king was Ahab, one of the most evil kings that have lived and, the Queen, the most evil queen, so evil that to this day, her name Jezebel is used when speaking of evil.

Their kingdom was the ten northern tribes of Israel.

We are told Obadiah (not a priest) had been a true believer in God since a child, and he was working in this evil situation, so evil that the king and queen had killed the true prophets of God because they spoke out against the worship of Baal and other false gods from the Canaanites.

It was in this wicked time Obadiah took his very life in jeopardy and hid one hundred true prophets of God in two caves, bringing them food and water, not just for a few days but possibly for three years.

I know there were many days his faith was tested. Would this be the day he was found out? Obadiah was just an ordinary man going to his job and being obedient to God.

Not much is known about him. We don't know what happened to him.

We learn a great prophet Elijah performed God's miracle after this, and I believe those one hundred true prophets were able to go out among the people with truth.

So next time you think your job is difficult, think of Obadiah.

HOW GOD SPEAKS TO ORDINARY PEOPLE | 77

Just as Obadiah was forgotten by men but not God, so God will never forget your faithfulness in your job and what you have been called to do (1 Kings 18).

PATTY

Walking down the hallway to visit with my husband in the nursing home, I saw her.

Sitting in her wheelchair, the first thing I noticed was she was too young to be there, just in her sixties with a long braid down her back, waiting by the nurse's cart for her medicine.

As I approached her, I smiled and said, "God loves you."

Her reply almost knocked me off my feet. She, with anger, said, "I know He loves to torture me."

I determined then I would greet her each day with a smile and say hello. As the weeks went by, going past her bitterness, I found she liked country music, so I brought her a CD player and music. Soon she started smiling at me. Wow, a breakthrough.

Not long after that, my husband was moved to the other end of the home, and I only saw her in the dining room. It was then God told me to tell Patty about salvation. Now how? She was bitter, quite mean to the nurses. So as I usually do, I started thinking up ways to approach her. I thought she would look good in pink, a great gift. God didn't let that happen, so next I planned (all this in my mind, of course), I would bring her a special meal in a private room and there tell her the plan of salvation. That didn't seem right either, but God kept telling me to tell Patty about salvation.

Then it happened, something that never had happened in a year. It was Sunday. I had been in church before I went to visit my husband. When I arrived, I was told he was in the therapy room. When I arrived, there he was by the bars, and there was Patty, all tied in to a machine. I sat down close where she was, and Scott, a Christian, knew I had been in church.

He asked, "What did your pastor speak on?" It was the plan of salvation, so I told Scott.

After exercise, I took my husband to the dining room, then to his room before I left to go home. I had driven about ten blocks and started laughing so hard I had to stop my car. There was Patty, all tied up to hear the gospel just as God had said I was to do.

After my husband passed to heaven, I continued going every week to see Patty. I asked her if I could pray for her. She said yes, but that was all. She told me she deserved to be there; it was her drinking. We became good friends. She even told me she loved me.

The last time I saw her was when I took her Christmas gift. I went on vacation, and Patty decided to stop going to dialysis, but before she died, another believer led her to salvation.

I will never ever forget nothing is impossible for God, even if He has to tie us up.

I am looking forward to seeing Patty again, healthy. What a day that will be. She never knew how much her life touched mine, how my faith grew being part of her life, and God's plan for both of us.

WHAT DO I DO NOW?

We may not know what God's plan for this country is, but we can know what God's purpose for all believers is. We are to stand firm in our trust of our God who knows the beginning of this nation, today, and what the future holds.

During this time of unrest in the nation, we are to view the culture through the lens of the Scriptures. To do this, we need to turn to the never-changing word of God and not to the limited wisdom of any man.

We are to seek His wisdom, pray for discernment, and obey God.

Remember, when we do as God has told us, take every concern to Him in prayer, talking about our problems to the one who has the power to change every situation. We must make sure we quit talking long enough to listen.

We have His promises in writing; believe them. When we don't trust them, we give up the peace and joy that Jesus said He will give us.

This country is in turmoil and suffering because we have turned from the true wisdom of God and listen to men of little understanding.

We are in war between good and evil. We can't live in God's kingdom and the culture of today. But just as spoken in the word, the battle is the Lord's.

So live your life in God's word, and His peace will be with you.

As King David said, "Yes, even in the valley of death there you are with me." And he should know; he faced many battles.

Take up your shield of faith and stand. Victory is ours in God.

WHAT DID THEY DO?

What did God want Abraham to do before Isaac was born?

What did God want Moses to do before He called him to go back to Egypt to lead His people out of slavery?

Tend sheep, get married, and work.

What did God want Daniel to do before He was called to stand for truth and was thrown into the lion's den? Live such a righteous life that his enemies couldn't find any fault in his work for the king.

All of the saints (ordinary people) in the Bible, both in the Old and New Testaments, were just like us. They married, had children, and worked, until God called on them to do unordinary service, some for a lifetime, and some for a period in time.

God knows who He is preparing for His service, like all of us ordinary people, just loving God and family, being prepared for His service seen or unseen, small or big. With God, no service is insignificant.

He has prepared us and has called us to be ready.

What a privilege when you think God, the great Creator, trusts us to be in His service.

Isn't it wonderful God doesn't call us to do great feats but just calls us to be faithful? Nothing is small in God's eyes when we obey; after all, isn't it God's approval, not man's we desire?

Sometimes we don't really see the people behind the events in the Bible, the ones God used to shape this world, people just like us.

So be thankful all us ordinary people because you see, we are God's children, loved, cared for, each with a Father who knows just what we need.

Wherever you are, God can and is using you. Aren't you thankful God has no favorites?

PLUM JAM

Fall is here with all the delicious fruit trees. I am fortunate to have a purple Italian plum tree. So at the right time, when the fruit was ready, so was I to make Plum Jam.

> 1 1/2 pounds of plums
> 1 1/2 cups sugar
> 1/4 cup of water
> 1/4 cup of lemon juice

The recipe told me to take out the seed and chop up the plums, so I put them in the blender, and was I surprised it was brown, not the purple I expected. It sure didn't look like it would turn out right.

Next I added the sweet sugar, but what I added next was sour lemon juice and water.

Placing the pan on the burner, I turned up the heat and let it boil. The longer it boiled (eighteen minutes), the more the beautiful purple was seen. It was the heat that did it. And it was the bitter lemon juice that made the jam set up and not run all over.

As I filled the two jam jars, I remember the promise God gave me when I was in the boiling pot of trial. He assured me He knew what He was doing and that He would never leave me to go through my pain alone.

Just as it took the sweet sugar and the sour lemon juice to make my jam, so does the blessings and trials of our life make us into what God has planned.

God gave us the gift of plums for our enjoyment that doesn't last, but God's gift of faith in Jesus is for eternity.

PS: The jam was delicious on toast but yummy on vanilla ice cream.

JAMES

There have been many Jameses in our world, but there is only one brother of Jesus named James. His life can be a great witness to us all.

I can imagine some of his thoughts. *Why didn't I see? Why didn't I believe?* and *How could I have said those things?*

Just as Apostle Paul must have many times thought, *How could I have killed those believers? Why didn't I understand the scrolls of scripture?*

They were human just like us, so you know there were times these memories plagued these men. We have the answer how they conquered these thoughts when they came to discourage them.

Paul said he viewed his past as filthy rags, but he strove ahead knowing his sins were forgiven.

James believed when Jesus came to him after His resurrection. Can you imagine what that meeting was like? Someday we too will have a meeting with our Lord.

Once, James knew Jesus only as his brother, but now he knew Him as his Lord.

James became the head of the believers in Jerusalem and was stoned to death in AD 62.

So never let your past control what your future can be.

Jesus is greater than your past and is the hope of your tomorrow.

BLINDERS

Before World War II, my father farmed with a team of horses, Hank and Nancy. They were older, well trained, and experienced. Since they were, their tack did not include blinders to keep them focused on what was ahead rather than to the side.

Some horses have to have hoods that cover their heads and ears to restrict crowd noises, allowing nervous horses to be ridden in parades.

These measures are especially helpful on younger horses.

It is time for true believers to focus on the Lord so they won't be distracted by the world around us but that they will become like Hank and Nancy just doing their work.

God has not given us blinders so we don't see and hear what is happening in the world around us, but He has given us armor to protect us from the clamor of the world. But it is up to us; it is a choice we make to put it on.

We are to be in the world, proclaiming God's gospel—His truth, His love, His promises—telling those in the world that Jesus came into this world that we might know His love.

So don't let the things of this world and the noise of the crowd distract you from faithfully doing the Lord's work, knowing there is a harvest yet to come.

God's armor, see Ephesians 6:10–19.

ASSURANCE

Do you need assurance? We all do.

We insure our homes and cars so we can have assurance if a disaster happens, we can replace them.

There was a man; his name was John. We know him as John the Baptist. There came a time he needed assurance too. He was in prison because of his faith, but in that dungeon, doubts plagued his mind. He did what we all should do. He sent his followers to ask Jesus, "Are you the one who was to come or should we expect someone else?"

Jesus sent word back about how the blind were receiving their sight, the lame were walking, the deaf received their hearing, and the Good News was being preached, and then the words, the very words John needed, "and blessed is the man who does not turn away."

After speaking these words, Jesus told the crowd, "Among those born of women there was no one greater."

So if you need assurance, you are among those Jesus called blessed. Do what John did. Go to Jesus. He will never turn you away. After all, He knows what we need (John 11:10).

GARAGE SALES

Andy Stanley said, "If you have a strong emotional desire, let that be a red flag before you make a decision." Good advice only if you apply it. I didn't.

After accepting the job of cleaning out a whole houseful and having a garage sale, I found out that red flag was well worth paying attention to.

Hours and days later, as the two-and-a-half-day sale was coming to an end, we made free piles. Some people would look through and accept our free offer. Others would look as we would invite them to take the items, but they would just walk by. Maybe they didn't want or need anything.

But how many people pass up what everyone needs, the most expensive gift ever given. I am speaking of the gift of salvation. The gift that cost Jesus His very life.

His gift is for everyone. Don't pass it up (John 3:16).

TURTLES

Turtles are another of God's spectacular creation. They live up to one hundred years, and all we see of them is their head, tail, arms, and legs.

There is an old fable about a turtle. One day in the forest, a rabbit comes up to the turtle laughing and said, "Do you ever get anywhere?" Full of pride, he bragged about all his talents and just how fast he was.

The turtle listened, then said, "I challenge you to a race."

All the forest creatures looked on. The race started, and Mr. Rabbit sped ahead. Looking back, he saw he was way ahead. So he sat under a tree for a rest. It wasn't long before he fell asleep. When he woke up, the race was over, and the turtle had won.

People are a lot like turtles and rabbits. Like a turtle, we are covered with a shell, our bodies. The real us is inside that no one sees. Like the rabbit, we can be so confident in our own ability we too can become prideful.

Mr. Turtle knew he couldn't win that race on his ability. It was his perseverance. Perseverance is a fruit of the Spirit.

Just as the forest creatures cheered the race on, the Book tells us we have a great crowd of witness cheering us too.

So just keep on; the race isn't over yet.

I AM NOT A FAN

Sorry, all you loyal fans out there. I'm not one of you. Maybe it's because I don't understand what's going on with all that running around, but I do know there is a *star*, the quarterback. It seems he is one big deal. People know his name and all his victories, but wait a minute. Isn't there a field full of men out there just following the plan? It seems it's to get that little ball to the end of the field.

Quarterbacks sure are important, but they couldn't move that ball without *the team*.

Just like us, we can be a star in our own mind, but we wouldn't be a pretty sight at the bottom of a heap.

So I guess the lesson is, we are in this together.

Go, team.

TREES

There is nothing like going to a tree, wiping off the fuzz, and biting into a peach so sweet the juice is running down your chin.

I love fruit and am blessed to have apple trees, cherry, pear, and plums.

Each of these has stories behind them. Take the peach tree. It produced a great crop until one winter. Snow and ice covered the ground. When spring came, I saw destruction. During those cold winter months, crawling under the ice and snow, the mice had ate all around the trunk and killed my tree. So I planted another. It grew, leafed out but stayed little, and after a few years, it didn't produce. So I found the reason; all the growth was aboveground, seen, but it had not established roots.

Then there were my plum trees; they grew. We watered, pruned, but didn't see but six plums. Every year for twelve years, I said next year, if they don't produce, I'm going to cut them down. You see, I had seen old battered trees loaded with fruit, and I just didn't understand why my trees looked strong, had beautiful leaves, but no fruit…It took fourteen years, and I had to call the neighbors to help pick all the big juicy purple plums.

Reminds me to be patient while my roots grow deep. As I let the Holy Spirit water me and prune me, I too will produce fruit of love, joy, peace.

Thank our loving Father who sees what we can become even when others can't.

SUBMIT

There is nothing that stirs our whole being more than seeing and hearing a single bugle playing taps over a coffin covered by the flag, a custom that was started during the Civil War. It doesn't matter if it is honoring a private or a general; they are soldiers.

Each soldier, no matter their rank, all learned one basic lesson—submit. They all know they are under the authority of someone with a higher rank.

As children, we marched and sang "I'm in the Lord's army." And as adults, we sing "Onward Christian Soldiers" (a song that was also written during the Civil War).

Just as our great men and women serve our country under the commander in chief, we must learn we also are under authority of one who not only is our great Creator but also the one who will one day announce with a trumpet "Now is the time I am bringing my soldiers home." The battles are over; the war is won.

Until then, remember who we serve.

PLEASURE

"Delight yourself in the Lord and He will give you the desire of your heart" (Psalm 37:4).

This is very personal; the word says *yourself*.

Delight means pleasure ourselves. What should we do? How do I find pleasure in the Lord?

We are told how. We look to the Lord—His mercy, faithfulness, power, love, and His promises—and remember all He has already done for us.

When we do this, He has promised He will give us the desires (strong wants) of our heart.

He said heart, not mind, because by dwelling in Christ, who He is, our hearts have been changed. Just as our minds have been renewed, now our desires and trust are in Christ, not just self.

God is a god of order. Look to His creation. First, the scripture says, "Delight yourself in the Lord," not that He gives us our desires. Oh, what a mess our lives would be if that was taken out of order. Instead, we are to take pleasure in God. *Then* His promise is He will give us what our renewed heart really desires—*His will*.

In 1922, Helen Lemmel wrote the song "Turn Your Eyes upon Jesus." The chorus says, "And the things of this world will grow strangely dim in the light of His glory and grace."

What a wonderful Savior!

TOO BUSY

The silent cry of the elderly: I know I'm loved. I know my physical needs have been met in the past and will be in the future. But what about my unspoken need? I understand you are busy, but just a small amount of your presence is missed. I want to know I matter.

But wait, is that the way I am with God? He knows I love Him. He knows I trust His care to provide for my needs. But what about my spending time with Him, just to be in His presence, speaking or in silence, just being with each other?

Does God's heart long for me, not fixing a problem, or a quick prayer spoken when I have a moment from a busy life?

Does God's heart long for just spending time with me?

One of the beloved hymns of the church speaks what our hearts need.

In the Garden

>I come to the garden alone
>While the dew is still on the roses
>And the voice I hear falling on my ear
>The Son of God discloses.
>
>And He walks with me and He talks with me
>And He tells me I am His own.
>And the joy we share as we tarry
>There none other has ever known.

(Written by C. Austin Miles, 1912)

We are never alone!

ANGER

I am angry.

I am angry when I hear of new laws passed to make recreational marijuana legal. I am angry when I hear it doesn't hurt anyone. If that is so, why do our children suffer even at their birth from the effects of drugs? I am angry when selfish mothers choose themselves over the welfare of their innocent yet-to-be-born child.

But wait! What about the other parents that would never take drugs while they are pregnant, some so diligent that they even eliminate coffee, yet these same loving parents that give them a stable home, good education, and material things withhold the most important of all, the very thing that we all need now and for eternity—instructions, bringing them up knowing the love of Jesus.

Some parents will spend time in the rain to watch them play, yet will not spend an hour in church.

Yes, I will admit I am angry or, should I say burdened, how good, loving parents are being deceived by the worldview of success.

It's good that our children can enjoy dance classes and all the outdoor sports; in fact, all children should have that opportunity. But what will that gain be if they become champions, have the acclaim of the world, and lose their souls?

Parents, wake up. You give and you give, and yet withhold the very thing they need the most—Jesus.

MEDITATION

Jesus's resurrection, really think about that. Not the word but what really happened.

He raised others from the dead while He was alive, and even after His death on the cross, He had the power to raise Himself to life. If I really believe that, what in this life of mine do I have to worry about?

And that is what Jesus is trying to tell us.

We read the Scriptures (God speaking) many times without doing as we are instructed. Meditate.

Reminds me growing up on the farm and looking out into the pasture. The cows would lie down and chew their cud. You see, they would first eat, but it didn't stop there. Later they would bring up what they had eaten and chew it again.

God says His Words are our spiritual food. Maybe we should eat and meditate, think, mull it over in our minds.

Be like the cows; enjoy and get all the nourishment you can, then lay down in the green pastures of God's word (John 2:19–22, Psalm 23).

LEARNING

Paul said he learned the secret of being content in any situation. As I read what he said, certain words reach out to me—*leaned, secret, content, any, I can, though, Him, gives strength.*

Wow! That's almost the whole verse. And so it is. We don't take out just what we want but all that was said for us. Like *learned*, it seems Paul was just like us. Some of life's biggest challenges are experiences that are not pleasant or onetime happenings but are over and over. Not what we want to experience, but it's a process, and some of us are slow learners.

The word *secret* is simply saying not everyone knows how to live a life of contentment. The secret is simple. Jesus told us it's His strength, not ours.

Then the word *through* is a great comfort. It makes me think of someone knocking on my door, and when I open it, they step through. That is what Jesus does.

Have a problem? As His children, when we face situations that seem we do not have the strength to be content, if we will just open ourselves, He will come into our hearts, and our weakness will be replaced with His strength.

The secret has been revealed. Give thanks; be content in the hard times knowing He takes you through. He is our strength.

Now that is joy.

I'M THANKFUL

Father, I am thankful you put David's sin and redemption in the Bible.

I'm thankful you told us of our father Abraham who took things in his own hands and made a mess of things.

Thank you for showing us when we rebel like Jonah, we can have a second chance. Like Moses, we're not too old to be used by you. Thank you.

Thank you for showing Rahab the prostitute was Jesus's ancestor.

Thank you that when Peter was overconfident and in his weakness denied you, oh how you forgave.

I'm thankful you revealed in your word how John the Baptist needed courage in that dungeon.

Paul, now what a turnaround; the murderer became Paul the Apostle to the Gentiles and proclaimed to us that he wasn't perfect but that he forgot the past and looked to the future.

Yes, Father, I'm thankful for these great men of faith, for they were just like me—forgiven!

TIME

How do you measure time?

We all have the same amount, eternity.

Whatever the amount you have left on earth, that is enough to complete God's purpose for you.

So make good use of your time, not just filling it with a busy schedule, so busy doing work (even good work) you don't take time to be who God created you to be, being content with what you already have.

Take time, shut off the noise, and listen to the sounds of God's creation. Now that's time worth taking.

New thought—the Lord Jesus was on this earth thirty-three years before the world knew Him. How long has it been since you took the time to know Him?

WAITING

There are rooms just for waiting—at the hospital, airport, and many establishments. Everyone there have one thing in common; they are all waiting for something.

We are told in the Scriptures to "wait upon the Lord." Does that mean we are to do nothing?

No, we are told to pray and seek God's will. So often, when we do, we go to God knowing what we want, and so often we ask Him to bless our will instead of seeking His will.

Seeking God's will takes time, time to let go of what we want and submit to what God wants.

I really believe when we have won that battle and have settled the question "God's will, not mine," the waiting just becomes easier.

As we wait and rest in confidence that God's will is the very best, today, tomorrow and forever, we have peace in God's promise. "I know the plans I have for you, plans to prosper you." And here's another, "No good thing does God withhold from us."

Keep on praying; the answer is on the way.

WRESTLING

Watching our children participate in sports is exhilarating. When they win or lose, no matter the outcome, they are winners.

Raising my children in the sixties, we, yes, we had wrestling matches; we called them Indian wrestling. Down on the floor we would go and try to throw each other with our legs.

Each child would say, "My turn, Mom, my turn," and they would challenge me to a match. Year after year, the challenge was on until the time came they could throw me over.

They never gave up. As their muscles grew, so their determination grew, and what a victory it was for them.

That is how we should face challenges in our lives. Keep the zeal; don't give up. Victory is waiting.

Wrestling has been around throughout the ages. There is a wrestling match in the Bible that will surprise you. Check it out in Genesis 32:24–30.

I NEED IT

God is teaching me (I'm a slow learner). I don't know as much as I think I do. In fact, I am learning I don't even know myself as well as I think I do.

All I have to do is look in the closet and see, hanging with all the others, what I was sure "I needed."

Watching TV, the commercial "I need it, and I need it now" convinces us sure enough we do.

It would be wonderful if my closet was my only lesson. Oh, no! Some have been much more expensive, spiritually and materially.

We have a wonderful counselor, the Holy Spirit. Now if we will learn from Him before we make that "I need it" decision, our lives and pocketbooks would be fuller.

So wait! Now that's an idea. Think—takes a little effort when "I need it" is going through our mind. But how much better off we would be when the new thought "no, I don't need that" is heeded.

During World War II, we had ration books. The back of mine said, "If you don't need it, don't buy it."

Good advice then, great advice now.

SEASONS

Living in the Northwest, we have definite seasons. Spring is full of new life. Where it seems there will be no flowers, the bulbs that lay dormant poke up through the ground, and soon, the beds are covered in the vibrant yellow of daffodils, then come the array of colors as the tulips come to life. Who can resist picking a bouquet of lilacs to bring in to set on the table? The birds are busy building their nests.

It seems all too soon, the newness of spring passes, and summer is upon us with the warm days. The grass needs mowed. The spring flowers are now replaced with roses and a wide variety of colors. The raspberries are hanging, and the strawberries are covering the ground. Our work increases, but so does the beauty.

In the fall, the air is crisp, and the leaves turn from green to yellow and a wide variety of colors. We know soon the harvest will be in, and the jars lining the shelf will be the provisions for winter.

It seems the year has passed quickly.

As the snow starts to cover the mountaintops, it won't be long until there will be no roses blooming, but they will be waiting for their time to bloom again come summer.

Yes, there is beauty in every season, just as there is beauty in each season of our lives.

In the spring of life, children are exploring the wonders of living. Once again it doesn't seem long until youth experiences adulthood that comes with all the responsibilities and joys. Fall, the family is raised, and we know winter is coming.

So don't miss the beauty of each season. When your hair (if you still have some) turns from rich brunette to white, and you no longer can do the things you once did, rejoice! Our spring is near.

As God promised, He will receive us unto Himself.

GUIDES

As we study the history of the expansion of the West, we learn it was full of extraordinary men and women, traveling to unseen places with a dream of a better life.

Some found what they were looking for, and others turned back when the journey became too hard.

My ancestors made that trek across the land to arrive in Montana before it became a territory. They did not set out on that journey without a guide. After they crossed the barren plains and swollen rivers then came to the mountains, it was their guide who brought them through.

So it is with us. We are making a journey. As we travel through our lives, we need a guide. Not just any guide but the Almighty God who traveled His journey on this earth. His name is Jesus. He has promised His Holy Spirit will be with us and guide us throughout our lives, until we reach the end of our journey, our home, with Him where we will be with Him throughout eternity.

SCALES

Sitting on my counter is an antique scale that my blind (yes, blind) great-grandfather used in his store. Its only purpose was to weigh things. It is heavy with a basket and weights.

He would fill the basket, and weights would tell the weight of what was in the basket.

What was put in the basket was important. It is like our minds and heart. When our circumstances become hard, we can put fear or trust on the scales.

Trust and fears are opposites. The less we have of one, the more we have of the other.

The secret to less fear is more trust in our Lord. Seek God in your distress. The more we know God, the more we trust Him. Look back where God has brought you from and know He promised He would be with us even through the valley of death.

We can trust Him to take care of all our todays, and when tomorrow comes, He will be there too.

It is written in Isaiah 12:2, "I will trust and not be afraid."

MECHANIC

All I know about how a car works is you need to keep oil and water in the engine, air in the tires, and gas in the tank.

So I was driving down the road, and all of a sudden, a message flashed. "Your engine has lost power." And sure enough, no matter how I pushed on the gas pedal, my car would not go any faster. The only thing I knew to do was pull over and get out the manual. There I found what I was to do. I could go a short distance to my dealer.

I was able to get home, and with visions of money leaving my purse, I called Dan, my mechanic.

When you know what to do, the difficult comes easy. With a little machine, the trouble was located. Of all things, a small sensor had failed in my gas pedal, which he fixed.

I am thankful I knew the right person to call. I knew my florist, medical doctor, or even my trusted pastor didn't know how to fix my problem.

There are many times we take our problem to the wrong person, like in the Bible when a young king asked for advice from his friends instead of wise advisors, and it caused his kingdom to fail.

So be careful whose advice you take. Yes, your best friend loves you, but do they know what you really need to get you back on the road with full power?

INSIGNIFICANT

We have all felt insignificant in the presence of something or someone at one time.

One of my hobbies of thirty years has been genealogy. My husband was not one bit interested as he said he was interested in the living, not the dead. But regardless, he patiently drove me around our state and encouraged me to travel across the states to gather my research.

I was blessed to find a copy of a journal written by my great-great-grandfather who was born September 22, 1834, in Nova Scotia. In his own writing, he spoke about leaving home at sixteen, learning carriage building, later traveling to Boston and learning carpentry. By 1856, he traveled for the Great West. He first took a steamer, the *Julia*, for Kansas at Saint Lewis, stopping in Saint Joseph where he stated he became engaged to a merchant by the name of Boney Wood. They crossed the plains for California. His duty was to count up and look after the stock of three hundred. The wagon train consisted of what he called three family ambulances loaded with women and children. First wagon was the Boney Wood family, then came seven Murphy wagons with five yokes of oxen pulling wagons loaded with provisions. That trip took six months. He spoke of the perils, how three were wounded by Indian arrows, but they did not lose one by death.

His story did not end there; he later traveled up into Canada. Later, on the fifth day of July 1860, he left by horseback for a six-week trip to what would become Montana Territory four years later.

When I read his journal, I thought about those five yokes of oxen. They were strong and steady as they prodded on. Even the Indians didn't try to steal them as they were insignificant to them.

They just wanted the horses. Only the pioneers knew their true value.

Sometimes we don't see the significance because we are too busy looking for the fancy prancing horses and forget what is most important.

In Matthew 11:29–30, Jesus said, "Take My yoke upon me for my burden is light."

WHAT DO YOU KNOW?

You have met one. I know I have. But help us, sometimes we are one too—a know-it-all.

Knowledge is wonderful. Without it, we would still be on horseback and cooking over a woodstove. But knowledge without wisdom and discernment can be destructive.

The Holy Scriptures tells us to seek knowledge and wisdom, but only when we learn to be obedient to what we learn will it matter in our lives.

The Scripture also tells us even a fool seems wise when he is silent.

Remember, don't be puffed up. Everything you know, you learned from someone else.

So let's keep on studying and learning as Tennyson said, "It's what we learn after we know it all that counts" (Proverbs 1:1–7).

TRAVELING

I have had the privilege of traveling to many places, from the desert to the mountains and flying to the islands, just enjoying the wonders of God's creation.

But I've never experienced what two men encountered.

I know the name of one of the men, Cleopas; the other, I don't. They were on a journey of about seven miles. As they walked, they talked of their discouragement and their hopes that had been shattered. Filled with grief, they traveled on. As they walked, another man joined them on the road. At the end of their journey, they invited the traveler to join them in a meal. And what a meal that was. You see, their companion was the risen Christ Jesus.

We have walked that road of discouragement; lost dreams and hopes have us burdened down. But just as the travelers on the road to Emmaus found hope, we do too. And just as the men, filled with joy, got up and returned to tell the wonderful news that Jesus was risen, so must we tell the news of the risen Savior.

So when you are discouraged, remember just as the Savior walked the road that day, He is still walking with us, giving us hope and peace that only His presence gives.

Keep traveling until you reach the end of your journey, then you will see the one that traveled with you even through the valley of the shadow of death (Psalm 23).

ACCOUNTS

I read of a story where some men were given money. Now that sounds great, but wait.

Some was given more than others. I don't know how I feel about that. Then I read how each was only accountable for what he had received.

My bank account may look smaller or bigger than others. I might live in a mansion or a tent. My life may seem worse or more blessed than others, but we all hold one thing in common; we have to give an account, sometimes on earth, but always when we stand before God.

I will never have to give account for what you have been given, only what I have. And that is more than enough accountability.

I often think of the tithes and offerings but forget the other blessings I have been given. My giving of money can be accounted for by my bank account, but what about my time and talents? I am to be faithful with my whole life. Sometimes only eternity will reveal what my time and talents have accomplished.

The Scriptures said even if we give a cup of water to a thirsty man, we have given to God.

Aren't you thankful you are not accountable for what God has given someone else? I sure am.

EXCUSES

Remember when Flip Wilson said, "The devil made me do it"? Funny, but not original. That was spoken thousands of years ago in the garden when a woman said the same thing. She wasn't alone that day. A man was there with his excuse too. He said that woman made me do it...and mankind has been making excuses ever since.

Some excuses can be quite original. As a teenager, I learned how to write as my father. That came in handy when I wanted an excuse why I wasn't in school. Probably just like Flip, that wasn't original either.

We may fool others with our excuses, but we can never fool God.

Until we come to God with no excuse or admit it wasn't just a mistake but a sin, will we find forgiveness.

The hymn "Just as I Am" that was written by Charlotte Elliot in 1834 says, "Without one plea, no excuses." Then just as God promised, when we confess with no excuse, His promise to forgive is ours.

So remember, no excuse is good enough. We must be honest with ourselves and honest with God, then and only then do we have perfect peace, the peace the world does not give, nor can it take away.

GAMES

As a mother, peekaboo was the first game I taught my babies. My heart soared with joy as I heard their laughter. It wasn't long before it was replaced with hide-and-seek. Their little bodies would hide behind a chair with their heads sticking out; they were just sure I couldn't see them. As they grew older, new games would be played.

We still play games, not innocent child games but games that end in tragedy, like trying to play hide-and-seek from God. Or peekaboo.

Now I love to play games, and winning is fun, especially when I can trump my grown grandchildren.

I'm sure Jesus played games when He was a child, and I can imagine he would race with Peter, James, and John.

So keep on playing, have fun, but remember, don't play hide-and-seek with God. You will never win.

WRAPPED IN LOVE

You probably have one. You know, the one no one but you see the value of. Its old, maybe out of style, but it has a special spot. Right there. Maybe on a shelf or in the corner of the room.

Hers was hanging in the closet.

It was her special day, and he couldn't be there. You see, God had taken him home. She knew she was loved, and everyone knew this too.

So what did she do? Over her beautiful wedding gown, she wrapped herself in his leather jacket, the one he wore for very special occasions.

Once again, she felt his love and knew she was forever loved by not just anybody but by her grandpa.

YELLOW BOOTS

Oh, what a beautiful morning; what a beautiful day. The sky is blue, and the sun is shining through my windows.

Oh no, there is a cloud, and more are forming. What shall I do? Drops of rain are falling.

I know, I'll get my umbrella. Now where did I put it? There it is, right where I put it by my chair. I'll just open it up and walk out into the rain.

My umbrella is the word of God. It won't stop the storm, but it will protect me from the rain. Maybe I should put on my yellow boots and sing in the rain.

SLIVERS

Living in the Northwest has much to offer. Going to the forest and getting wood is one of my favorite activities.

After dressing appropriate, and the pickup is loaded with chain saw, cables, gas, and oil, the preparations are ready. With permit and snacks, we head out.

The forest is a haven of quiet; the air is brisk and fresh. As the wood is cut, the fragrance is better than any perfume I own.

Now I'm not strong enough to do the falling and cutting, so loading the pickup is my job.

After a hard day of work, with achy bodies, home we go with a deep satisfaction, knowing we will be warm come winter.

The other day, I put on my boots that I had worn, and a sliver went into my foot.

That reminded me about a scripture that says we can't take the sliver out of someone's eye when we have a log in ours.

Ouch, that really hurts because I try that sometimes myself. I need to also remember the rest of the scripture that tells me to first remove the sliver from my own eye before I can help someone else.

SNOW

As I look out my window, the sun is coming up over the mountain peak. The snow is glistening like little diamonds. The birds are swapping and gliding across the blue sky.

I find the ground covered with snow, beautiful, but to the birds, it is a challenge. No way does the early bird get the worm, but somehow, they are eating, building their nests, singing, and just trusting their Creator.

As I ponder this picture, I remember God tells us to consider the birds. When life is a challenge, consider what the birds know.

Spring will come, and the ground once again will yield up its blessing.

So keep on singing and trusting our great God who provides all of His creation's needs.

Even mine!

AN OPEN HEART

As we go through our lives, God gives His children many lessons that do not come from the pulpit or our daily devotions.

The estate sale I was holding was busy. I noticed the quiet man as he picked up the crystal figurines, examining them in the light. I soon was busy helping an older lady. She carried her blue Pyrex dishes over to my table to pay for them, all the time telling me how beautiful they were. She opened her purse, counted her money, and said she would put them back because she didn't have enough to pay for them.

And then standing behind me, I heard a quiet voice saying, "I will pay for them."

I looked at him and said, "Would you like to tell her?"

He said, "No, you tell her."

I did. She turned to him and said thank you and left.

Now we were alone, and I told him, "That was a very nice thing you did." I smiled at him and said I am shy too.

He said, "I don't like to talk to people. I have PTS. While serving in Iraq, it was my job to train the Iraqi soldiers." He dropped his head and quietly said, "Some of those same soldiers turned on our army and killed some of us, and I just can't forget I am the one who trained them."

He moved away from me, looked around some, and returned to pay for his small crystal figurines. I told him I will never forget you and your kindness. He shyly smiled and walked away.

Out of his hurt and pain, with a heart so tender, he saw beauty in small crystal figurines and gave to a little lady because she saw beauty in blue Pyrex dishes.

Oh, God, give me a heart like his to see past myself and give like that quiet, gentle man.

WHO KNOWS YOU?

Some people know him by his grill, others by his boxing. I am speaking of George Foreman.

I know who he is by both, but there is something else I know about him because I experienced it.

While traveling, I had the opportunity of meeting him. What a friendly and courteous man he was.

As the crowd was invited to have their picture taken with him, I went forward and sat beside him. His muscles were the size of my thighs, but that wasn't what made the biggest impression on ne.

When I sat down, he spoke and looked at me as though he knew me, someone he'd never seen and would never see again.

Jesus assures me He knows me, and because of His love for us, He gave us the gift of the Holy Spirit so we can know Him. As the Bible tells us, "I know My sheep and My sheep know me" (John 10:14).

WE ALL FALL

As a parent, we didn't rush in and stop our toddlers from falling. We didn't keep them from trying by always holding them.

Yes, they got hurt, and we would kiss them and let them keep trying.

School years came, and we didn't do their homework so they wouldn't fail. We didn't and couldn't study for them.

And now our children are grown and raising their families, and once again, we can't step in and do for them what they must do for themselves.

If we as humans know this, why do we expect God will not allow troubles to come our way that He knows will produce faith and strength?

What a wonderful Father we have. Just as His eyes are on the sparrow that falls, so He is with us always to lift us up when we fall, He teaches us His words, and someday, He will bring us home.

Never, never stop. If you fall, get up, until that wonderful day when we will be home with our Father.

What a day that will be.

WHOSE PLAN?

God has a plan for our lives. He has equipped us. Do we mess up? You bet, we do. But God's plan did not change. You see, He knew us before we were born. He knew how we lived and how we now live. He knows when we will draw our last breath.

Yes, God has a plan. He makes all things work together, the good and the bad. Yes, all things.

Our God is in control. We can praise our Lord because He had and still has a plan. No second best for His children but God's best that He had for us in the beginning. Jesus said and says today, "I know the plans I have for you, plans to prosper you."

Sometimes I get so busy thinking about my plans I don't take time to listen to God's plans for me.

What a mighty God. He created us. How marvelous! He loves us.

At salvation, He came into our innermost being by His Holy spirit to teach us and guide us. He has equipped us to fulfill His plan for our lives.

If that doesn't bring peace and joy, whatever could!

STORMS

There is a storm outside, with thunder and lightning. The trees are bending as the wind whips them around. Rain is pelting my window.

Where am I? Inside. I can see the storm, but it is not touching me.

Like our storms of life. They come as our circumstance change from sunny skies to thunder, but the Holy Spirit is with us inside, and when we have to step out into the storm, the Holy Spirit is stepping out with us.

As the storm passed, all became calm; the wind and rain stopped. The clouds were still in the sky, but the sun was beginning to peak through.

Yes, there was some damage, but the storm passed.

Reminds me of the song "Till the Storm Passes By" written by Mosie Lister. The last words in the chorus can be our prayer: "Hold me fast, let me stand in the hollow of thy hand / Keep me safe till the storm passes by."

Oh, and remember, this storm too will pass.

Until then, hold on to His almighty hand.

DON'T WORRY

When we are told "don't worry," we don't have the power to make the trouble go away.

But when Jesus said "do not fear," He has the power to change the situation or to calm our fearful thoughts until our fear is replaced with peace.

God knows right where we are, and He is present with us, the All-Powerful Eternal Father and our Lord Jesus who loved us so much that He shed His blood for every one of us, even me.

If He is for us, who or what can prevail against us as the Holy Spirit guides us, sustains us, and will be present in us to bring us through even this our present trial?

Until then, the beloved song "Through it All" can be our song of praise.

Andre Crouch wrote this blessed hymn from experience. Within two years, he lost his father, mother, and brother. Later he suffered from cancer and congestive heart failure.

We all have had many struggles and hardships, but like Andre, we have a Savior who is there through it all.

LIGHT

Isn't it interesting that darkness can't overcome light, but light can overcome darkness? Try it.

Where can you find darkness to sit on your table to take away light? But we know we can light a candle, place it on our table, and light will take away darkness.

I love my night-light; no matter how dark, I can find my way. When morning comes, light pours through my windows, and I can see clearly all around me. Ah, but wait, look at lightning as it flashes across the stormy sky.

God thought light was so important He created two great lights, the sun and moon.

Jesus said He is the light of the world that casts out the darkness. We can walk in that light when we let Him cast out the darkness in our life.

No matter, whether the light is just a small night-light or the sun-filled day, He can light our way. We too are to be a light to those around us. Just as the moon reflects the light of the sun, we too can reflect the light of the *Son*.

LESSONS FROM MP3 PLAYER

It was all charged up and ready to play, and it did beautifully. Then it just quit. No warning; it just up and stopped playing. It couldn't play anymore. All the power was used up.

I am just like that. I have no power that I don't get every day. I am speaking of the power from the Holy Spirit. It is then I can sing loud, but I must remember I have to go back every day to the same Power source, or I am dead, unable to sing a note. But when I do, I have pleasant music that God has placed in me to encourage me, help me, oh yes, and dance too.

Remember where your power is little MP3 player.

ORDINARY

Today is not an ordinary day!

It is a new day, one we have never had before and will never have again.

It is a new day blessed by God.

Today I will go about the day doing ordinary chores. My bed needs to be made, meals cooked, and a family to look after, a job to go to.

But it is no ordinary day.

You see, my beloved Father woke me up with new words, just for me, just for today. He has promised "my blessings are new every morning." And when God blesses, every ordinary day becomes no longer ordinary because we can carry His words with us throughout the day. And when we shut the light out at night, we have His promise in Psalm 139, "I know when you lay down."

Now what is ordinary about that!

PONDERING

There are some things I don't understand that causes me to stop and think and think again.

There is a situation in the Bible that has me thinking and wondering about.

Samuel 24 tells about a war that had been going on for years. King Saul was hunting down David, an innocent man.

So one day, as David was hiding in the back of a cave, King Saul came in for privacy to relieve himself. David's men saw this as a great opportunity to end this war. They told him, "God has placed him in your hands kill him." David did not.

Why? It sure seemed God had delivered Saul. It couldn't be plainer, could it? Even his soldiers encouraged him, those faithful men who had stood beside him.

What was it that David knew? He knew he was an innocent man. He knew God had anointed him to be the king. But is this the time? Is this how God's plan to place the kingdom in his hands was to be? Questions.

I have asked myself all those questions, and I still don't know, but David did, and that's all that matters.

Saul was not David's enemy, even though David was Saul's.

The Lord tells us it is not for us to take revenge. Maybe that is what David knew.

I want a heart that knows when the circumstance and friends tell me one thing, but my Savior reveals what He would have me do. I want to obey like David did.

God said in Scripture, "Obedience is better than sacrifice."

HOW MUCH DO YOU KNOW?

As we study the Scriptures, we often see just a part, usually the spectacular, and we don't see a clear picture of God working in a human life.

If we were asked about a man called Elijah, most of us would tell how he went to Mount Carmel and how fire fell from heaven, and the prophets of Baal were killed. Then we would remember how God took him up to heaven in a chariot.

But who was he? Why is that all we remember?

Once again, as the Scripture reveals, he was living his life east of the Jordan River when God called and directed him to go to the wicked king Ahab and pronounce God's judgment on the land for the worship of idols, the judgment of no rain on their crops for three years.

He obeyed and, because of this, risk God-sent Elijah to hide in a ravine, a deep gully, where God supplied his food and water. He probably wondered why the creek was drying up when God had told him He would supply him. It was after the creek dried up God told him to go to a foreign land, Sidon (now Lebanon). There God supplied his needs, not by a woman of wealth but a poor widow.

Later, a year or so, God said, "Go back to the man that is looking to take your life." He obeyed.

It was then after years he returned the miracles of Mount Carmel happened.

One of the things we learn from this part of Elijah's life is God didn't give His prophet the full picture, just step-by-step, just as He does for us.

But the victory became the beginning of the run for his life. Fear overtook him. Just as we can be overcome with fear, so did he, and just as God didn't condemn him, neither does God condemn us. Just as God provided what Elijah needed, so He does for us.

Great news after God spoke to him again; Elijah returned to the work God planned for him. Years later, after faithful service, God transported him to heaven in that chariot.

I'm quite sure we aren't going to be taken up to heaven in a chariot, but God said, one day. we who are still alive will meet Him in the air.

So be obedient, step-by-step, day by day. That's how all God's people lived.

GERITOL

Years ago, there was a popular commercial.

> Are you tired, run-down? Lack of energy? Just take Geritol. In just 24 hours, you will feel stronger and with more energy.

I have a question to ask.

Are you tired, run-down, feel drained spiritually?

Don't add more religion; return to God. It is then you will renew your strength and soar like an eagle.

God gave a message to the church in Revelation 2:4–5. He told them, "You have forsaken your first love. Remember the height from which you have fallen, repent and do the things you did at first and God will restore you."

Trying to live in the secular world and living in the spiritual world is exhausting. We are double-minded and unstable. But when we live each day as God directs, we are at peace.

Yes, our bodies can get tired, but we are promised new blessings each morning. So don't rely on Geritol that they promised would give iron to your blood.

Just return to your first love. His name is Jesus, He that gave His blood, that restores our souls now and forever.

HAPPY TRAILS

God founded only one nation, Israel, and we are a nation founded on a constitution that reflects God's moral law. The freedoms we have are unlike other nations. Our prosperity is unknown and envied all around the world. But we are no longer the nation our forefathers gave their lives, liberty, and fortunes to establish. Our freedoms are being destroyed.

It is the church (the believers) living in apathy that has stood by and watched as the culture we live in has eroded because we have not stood up and spoke up and lived up to our faith.

We need to ask ourselves, am I living by what I confess to believe? If I continue living as I am now, will I be closer to God, or will I become more like the culture around me?

Remember, our life is like a mist, here today, gone tomorrow, and this world will also pass away. So how should we live? By knowing God's word that never changes, but it will change us.

Believe God; set your heart and mind on God's promises. Meditate on His history throughout time. The more you know the *true* God, the more you will understand, and you will start to see through the Holy Spirit's eyes.

We must remember, faith is not a feeling or emotion; it is simply believing what God has said, and if God said it, *it will happen*.

God has a wonderful plan for us. A great prophet in the Bible said, "When everything falls, I will stand with God." That should be our confession too.

In the years 1951–1957, Roy Rodgers and Dale Evans had a popular Western program. Their theme song was "Happy Trails." Some of the words were "Some trails are happy ones, others are blue / It's the way you ride the trail that counts." The last words were "Just sing a song and bring the sunny weather / Happy trails to you until we meet again."

We might not be on a trail ride, but we are making a journey through this life, and we know as God's children, we are never alone.

In the 1950s, Jim Hill wrote a song. "What a day that will be when my Jesus I shall see / When I look upon His face, the one who saved me by His grace / Then forever I will be with the one who died for me / What a day, glorious day that will be."

So, fellow traveler, keep the faith. Very soon we will be with our wonderful Lord.

THIRTY YEARS

As we look back at our lives, we can see a lot of changes. Some are good, and some changes are bad.

There are some things that haven't changed, but there have been many. Our families have changed—marriages, new babies born, and even the death of loved ones.

Scripture tells us in Revelation of a church that changed as a warning to us. It didn't change for the better but for the worse.

The church was located in Laodicea, a very wealthy banking town located on trade routes. Many people would come into the town for the hot springs that flowed down into the city. It was under the control of Rome, but now in modern-day Turkey.

The church was established by Epaphras, a coworker of Paul.

Paul, writing in Colossians 2:1, told how he was struggling with his concern for them. Paul himself was in prison for his faith, yet his concern troubled him, not because they were undergoing persecution but because of those that were creeping into the church. It appears they were a wealthy church and felt they had no need for anything.

Later, just thirty years or so, we read in Revelation 3:14–21 what had been happening.

In the letter to the church that Jesus had John write and send them, it revealed the true church.

He said, "I know what you have become, neither hot nor cold." They thought they were rich, but Jesus told them, "You are poor and naked." They were also told they made Jesus sick.

But because of God's great mercy and grace, He told them if they earnestly repented, He would come into their church.

I don't know if or when the church repented, but we are told in history a great earthquake destroyed the city, and only a few remains can be seen. But this we know, Jesus said, "The gates of hell cannot stop His church," and we are witnesses to that. His church is here thousands of years later.

God is full of grace and mercy. For that we can be thankful, but God also wants His church, His believers, to be earnest, not part of the culture but a light to the unbelieving world.

Just thirty years. What a lesson for us.

NOVEMBER 3, 2020

As I am writing, the voting has begun. We don't know the outcome, but by the time you read this, we will.

Knowing our nation was at a crossroad, many faithful ministers called out; just as John the Baptist did in the wilderness. "Repent and turn back to God."

Many heeded that call as thousands filled the Washington mall and churches on many occasions, heeding God's words, "If my people, who are called by my name will repent and turn from their wicked way, I will restore their nation."

Israel in Bible times would do the same. When trouble invaded their land, and they were living under threat, they called out, and God delivered them.

For a while, the people would, but soon, they returned to their own way.

Time after time this happened, until God said, "You honor me with your lips, but your heart is far from me," and He removed them from the land.

After 9/11, people filled the churches and called on God. Once again, very soon, we went back to our own ways.

We too honored God with our lips, not our hearts. Now just a few years later, we called out to God.

Did we in true repentance, or did we honor God with just our lips?

Did we put our trust in a man, political party, or did we put our trust in God alone? God knows our hearts.

I pray He will have mercy on our country.

FORT ELLIS

Fort Ellis was an army fort established in 1867 east of Bozeman, Montana. It was named after Colonel Ellis who was killed in 1863 at the battle of Gettysburg.

Troops from the fort were responsible in many campaigns of the Indian wars. It was to protect the settlers and miners. The fort was eventually closed in 1886. Most of the soldiers belonged to the cavalry.

There were many forts scattered throughout the country as safe havens for the nearby people to run to in times of danger. We can read of these sanctuaries of safety in the history books and see some of the remains.

We are in a war. Every generation since Adam and Eve has had an enemy. It is the battle between good and evil, between God and His people and the enemy, Satan.

Our enemy isn't pretending anymore or hiding in the shadows. All we have to do is look at our culture today. What was once called evil is called good, and what was called good is now called evil.

We have a stronghold that we can go to in times of trouble. His name is Jesus, our Savior.

Just as the soldiers went outside to work, so must we. There are battles to fight, but the war is already finished at the cross.

Our homes should also be a place of peace and safety, a place of refuge from the world.

With God, our stronghold is where His peace and strength are, not just nearby but in us.

Aren't you thankful that we have a place of safety where the enemy can't destroy us? All we have to do is go to God.

Day after day, God is in control. God wants us to live in the safety of His love. Fort Ellis is long gone with all the soldiers, but our Stronghold is with us forever.

Note: The sheriff was John C. Guy (my great-great-grandfather).

AFTER ELECTION

The day came and went, and the results are not clearly known.

But what is important is that we know God is in control. What really matters is where I put my trust.

We know God has a plan for this world from the beginning of creation to the end of the age.

Scriptures tells us, as the time of the end comes, the righteous will get more righteous, and the wicked more wicked.

We should not be surprised when some people say the Constitution is not relative for the day. They have already said God's word isn't either. They have taken God out of the culture of today and replaced it with relativism.

All that is happening maybe beyond our understanding, but it is not beyond our faith in the one true God and our Savior, Jesus. We must pray for faith and be obedient to God's word, even when we don't understand.

We can be sad when we know how our nation is turning more and more from the Constitution and what our Constitution was based on.

We must not deny reality, but it is not any political party that will restore our nation but God alone. Just as Jeremiah in the Old Testament was known as the weeping prophet because he saw his nation turn from God and saw the destruction, so we weep for our country.

But just as Jeremiah put his trust in God and was obedient, so must we.

His message to the people was "Repent and turn to God," so we should proclaim the same message. But we must also tell people Jesus will return. He is our hope.

"The Lord gives His people strength. The Lord blesses His people with peace" (Psalm 29:11).

Just as Queen Esther was told by her uncle Mordecai, "Who knows but that you have come to this royal position for such a time as this," we hold a royal position as children of the King.

Other believers in their time have come and gone, most forgotten today, but not by God. They lived in turbulent times, just as our brothers and sisters in other nations are. Our nation is in turbulent times, but God has chosen each of us to remain steadfast and true to His words without compromise.

Jesus is Lord.

PROMISED LAND

When God promised Abraham that his descendants would inherit the land he was living on, it was occupied by the Canaanites. He was also told his descendants would be held in captivity for over four hundred years before they would.

Just as God promised, His people were led out of Egypt, where they had been held as slaves for 430 years.

As they were led through the Red Sea and came to the border, Moses sent twelve men, one from each tribe of the Hebrews, as representatives to spy out the land. When they returned, ten men saw that the land was filled with plenty, but they also saw the giants in the land, and they did not believe that God was able to keep His promise. Two men, Joshua and Caleb, saw the same circumstance, but they reported, "God is able." Because of unbelief, the people did not cross over but wandered around in the desert for forty years as a punishment to those who had known of God's miracles but did not believe. (We must be careful who we listen to.) Even then, God, in His mercy, provided them everything they needed. Manna, bread was there every morning and quail in the evening; their clothes didn't wear out. Even in their unfaithfulness, God was faithful.

Once again, they came to the border. They again knew the Promised Land lay just ahead.

Now, once again, two men were sent. They saw the land; they saw the people, but also heard how afraid the people were of them because they knew their God was with them. One woman, Rahab, a prostitute who had only heard, believed what the Israelites had heard and seen. Rahab was so blessed; because of her belief, she was rescued, and she became an ancestor of Jesus.

When under the leadership of Joshua, the Israelites crossed over the Jordan. He told them, "Keep your eyes on the Ark [God's presence]. You have never been this way before."

That very day, they crossed over and ate of the produce of the land the Manna stopped.

Yes, they had fought battles of defense before. They had conquered some kings, but now they were to fight in offense and take the land. God went before them.

When we think of the Promised Land God gave to them, we read of the plenty, but now they had to work the land that God provided.

So it is with us as believers. God delivered us out of the slavery of sin and bondage. He promised He will take us to the Promised Land. Just as He promised, he would be with them; we have that same promise. Just as they encountered battles, so do we.

God's instruction to them is the same to us, "Be not afraid, be not discouraged." Yes, we have battles ahead, but we also have God's promise, "I will never leave or forsake you."

Soon, we too will make a crossing to the other side; what a glorious day that will be!

WHAT HAS FAILURE GOT TO DO WITH IT?

We all have failed and have regrets, but do they hold us back?

There was a young man raised in a God-believing home. It was a home of a relative wealth for the day. A large enough home to hold 120 people, with a young servant girl named, Rhoda. The young man's name was Mark and called John Mark.

Mark had seen Jesus being led from the garden. In fear, he fled for his life, just as the others did.

What turmoil followed after the crucifixion? James, the brother of John, was killed, and when the authority seen how it pleased the Jewish leaders of the day, they arrested Peter and put him in a cell, expecting to call him the next day. But our God sent an angel in the middle of the night and led him out. Mark's mother, Mary, was holding a prayer meeting, asking God to protect Peter, and He did. Mark had a wealthy Levite cousin, Barnabus, that was a follower of Jesus and a fellow worker with Apostle Paul.

The time came that young Mark was asked to go on a missionary journey as a helper, with Barnabus and Paul. It was a long journey filled with many miracles and trials. Sometime later, in Perga, he deserted them to go back home. He had failed.

A second trip was planned, and Barnabus wanted Mark to go with them again. Paul was so against it that an argument arose. Paul chose another man, and Barnabus took Mark.

The scriptures do not tell us when Paul and Mark reunited, when Mark humbled himself, and when Paul forgave Mark, humbled himself and asked to serve together again.

We are told in Philemon 1:24, "Mark and Paul were together in Rome."

When Paul was an old man, he wrote to Timothy and asked him to bring Mark to him because he was useful to his ministry. Paul also recommended him to the church in Colossian.

Not many of us will see our failures told down through the years. Mark himself told of his as did other writers, but praise is to God who raised him up to be a strong leader during turbulent times.

It is written, "He who began the good work in us will finish the good work in us." So don't let your failures define you. Jesus isn't finished with you yet.

There are outside of the biblical records that tell us Mark was dragged to death for his faith. From failure to faith, that is how we can remember Mark.

SUNDAY MORNING

How long has it been since you went to church with Thanksgiving in your heart? Since in praise you said, "This is the day the Lord has made. I will rejoice and be glad in it."

Most of us do not know what our ancestors did generations ago but let me tell you of one family. This family was from the tribe of Levi and the descendant of a famous cousin we know as Moses.

When we read the scriptures of Moses, we find more than the crossing of the Red Sea and the receiving of the Ten Commandments, but a family that was not just saintly.

Moses's brother, Aaron, built a golden calf and lied about it. His older sister and Aaron resented Moses and wanted to be in control. And his cousin, Korah, led a rebellion against him with 250 men, and the Lord caused them all to be swallowed up by an earthquake.

When we turn to the Psalms, we learn that generations later, because of God's unfailing love, we can read of the sons of Korah. Let me share a portion of what they have written to sing. "As a deer pants for streams of water so my soul pants for you, o God" (Psalm 42). "Put your hope in God, He knows the secrets of our hearts" (Psalm 44). "God's throne will last forever" (Psalms 45). "God is our refuge" (Psalms 46). "How awesome is the Lord the Great King" (Psalms 47). "For God is our God" (Psalms 48).

The sons of Korah were gatekeeper's composers and singers in the tabernacle and later in the temple of Jerusalem.

When we turn to Psalm 84, we read what they have written, and our hearts rejoice. "How lovely is your dwelling place, O Lord Almighty. My soul yearns even faints for the courts of the Lord. My heart and my flesh cry out for the living God. Even the sparrow has found a home, and the swallow a nest for herself, where she may have her young a place near the altar. Blessed are those who dwell in your house. They are ever praising you." At the end of the Psalm, they tell us how they rejoiced. "Better is one day in your courts than a thousand elsewhere." And then said, "We would rather be a doorkeeper in the house of God than dwell in the tents of the wicked."

Can't you just picture the joy as they see the bird raising her young by the altar? Can't you just feel the contentment and wonder of being a doorkeeper in God's house.

We are so blessed to have these Psalms to remind us of the greatness of God and what a privilege it is to enter His house.

ABOUT THE AUTHOR

Georgia Wagner Branscome is a fifth-generation Montanan. She was born in 1939 on a rural farm in Kalispell, Montana, now living one mile from the farm she was raised on. She is a member of the Kalispell Church of the Nazarene, the church she attended as a child. She still enjoys the beauty of the Northwest, gardening, music, family, and the study of the Scripture. If asked, she would tell you peace and joy is hers as she lives with the promise God gave her: "I know the plans I have for you." She is blessed to have a close and caring family of three children and their spouses, seven grandchildren and spouses, and fifteen great-grandchildren.